P9-DEH-853

ADVERTISING: REFLECTIONS OF A CENTURY

ADVERTISING

Reflections of a Century

Bryan Holme

A Studio Book

The Viking Press New York

To
my darling and very patient
Elfrida

Copyright © 1982 by Bryan Holme
All rights reserved

Published in 1982 by The Viking Press
(A Studio Book)
625 Madison Avenue, New York, N.Y. 10022
Published simultaneously in Canada by
Penguin Books Canada Limited

Library of Congress Cataloging in Publication Data
Holme, Bryan, 1913–
   Advertising, reflections of a century.
   (A Studio book)
   1.   Advertising—History.   I.   Title.
HF5811.H65   659.1'09   82-70186
ISBN 0-670-74728-9   AACR2

Printed in Japan

Design by Christopher Holme

INTRODUCTION

This history is a panoramic view of the last hundred years as seen through the eyes of that keen and concerned observer of society —the advertiser. In presentations of food, clothing, housing, cigarettes, cosmetics, liquor, new inventions, travel, sport, art, and entertainment, we see how we have looked, lived, and thought from the days of the gaslit café to those of the disco, from the early years of automobiling, 'floating hotels', and experimental aircraft to the age of space and computers.

The illustrations, selected from many thousands of advertisements, posters, and covers, represent the work of some of the greatest artists and photographers in the field. The level of aesthetics is therefore very high. Yet almost without exception even the most esoteric or prestigious of these ads appeared in major newspapers, national weeklies, or monthly magazines, and the posters received wide exposure on the billboards. They show not only how prominent manufacturers, quality retailers, travel, utility, and other services have reflected the taste of each decade in successful advertising, but in some of the more brilliant campaigns how they actually helped influence that taste.

Too many years have passed for even the most senior of citizens to remember the days when the posters of Jules Chéret were the toast of Paris, when Toulouse-Lautrec was sketching at the Moulin Rouge and the Divan Japonais, when cat lovers awaited the next Steinlen poster as eagerly as Sarah Bernhardt's fans scanned the hoardings for Mucha's newest portrait of the actress. And it is well over ninety years since Pears caused outcries in London's academic circles by acquiring Millais' famed 'Bubbles', a portrait of the artist's grandson, and using it to advertise their soap—so successfully too! Yet these and other examples of the 1880s and 1890s are more widely known today than are many later milestones in advertising art. Not only were posters of this 'golden age' avidly collected until shortly after the turn of the century (which, incidentally, explains why so many of these perishable lithographs still exist), but, fanned by recent magazine articles, exhibitions, by auction sales and the appearance of book after book about posters, the interest in this popular art form has never been greater than now.

To many readers, therefore, what followed in the Edwardian era, between the two World Wars, and two or three decades after may be less familiar and proportionally more rewarding.

Each decade had a spirit, a look, a mood of its own which is reflected in its advertising: the lingering Edwardian elegance of the 1910s, for instance, the emancipated, art deco, yet 'pretty' look of the twenties, the sober, increasingly art-conscious mood of the 'depressed' thirties—and so on through the war-torn forties, affluent fifties, rebellious sixties, to the computerized, jean-crazy seventies of recent memory. Each said something new—or at least said the old in a new way.

Apart from the telltale face of some famous personality endorsing a face cream, soap, or other product, or an ad that is connected with a well-known event and thus tied to a specific date, it's the style of clothes people are wearing, the type of architecture shown, the way a room is decorated, or the shape of an automobile, refrigerator, telephone, or other familiar household object that will quickly date an illustration. The final clue to a period is the artwork itself—the conception, the manner in which the subject is posed, the style of an illustration.

Advertisements, posters in particular, have often been called the art of the poor man. It costs no more to look at a good poster than a bad one, but as often as not even a good poster is glimpsed through the window of a train, car, taxi, or bus, in passing and in less than ideal surroundings. Knowing this, the poster artist aims to achieve instant contact with the viewer, so the advertiser's message—perhaps no more than a single word—hits him at first glance. Even so, a speeding vehicle allows little leisure for the enjoyment of the poster itself.

In much the same way the well-designed newspaper or magazine ad can suffer from its surroundings, from ads with conflicting messages and aesthetics, which can bore, disgust, or otherwise hasten the turning of the page. But an ad or a poster taken on its own, mounted and exhibited with plenty of space around it, can be appreciated like any other work of art.

The wide scope of the book unfortunately ruled out the luxury of giving every illustration a full page, but none of the reproductions is too small to be enjoyed, and particular attention has been given to how well one example sits with the next. The wealth of available material called for a few further guidelines. Priority was given to colour over black-and-white and, in keeping with the theme of the book, to ads featuring people and activities rather than single object or still life compositions. The selection was limited almost entirely to English-language examples, with a few major French milestones. To spread the net as wide as possible, the attempt was made to restrict each advertiser, division, or subsidiary to one or, at the most, two examples of any one product. This was particularly difficult in the case of advertisers such as London Transport, Shell-Mex, The Container Corporation of America, Capehart Radio, RCA, De Beers, Schweppes, General Foods, Fortnum & Mason, Lever Brothers, Guinness, L.N.E.R., Gillette, and Johnson & Johnson. These represent a few of the companies to each of whose consistently brilliant advertising campaigns a whole book could, should, and sometimes actually has been devoted.

Finally, a word in praise of the unsung hero of this book—the advertising agent. Without the benefit of his talents, relatively few of the illustrations would be here to enjoy, or at least not in their present form.

In very general terms, the function of an agency—which usually consists of executive, creative, research, media, technical, and administrative departments—is to present to its client a new, catchy, and practical idea for a campaign, furnish an outline with mockups and estimates, and after final approval see the project through to the end. In the area of graphics, the art director—described ideally as a retail merchant at heart but one with great taste, flair, courage, and diplomacy—working in close cooperation with the copywriter and client, decides on the kind of illustration best suited to the selling theme, the product, and kind of image the advertiser wishes to project.

From then on, the art director's function can vary all the way from executing the artwork himself or finding someone else to carry out the idea he will probably have roughed-out on paper, to approaching a big-name artist, illustrator, or creative photographer and giving him anything up to carte blanche to produce

not 'pretentious acrobats' but otherwise nothing less than sensational results. But even then almost always it's up to other talents to design the lettering for the banner line, select the type for the message, put the whole ad together and ready it for the engraver. This point about teamwork is brought up to explain why in the following pages the name of the artist or photographer credited under each illustration—next to the year the ad ran—is sometimes missing. In a record of this nature, and where several talents may have been equally or almost equally responsible for the finished artwork, it has sometimes been the policy of the advertiser or agent to withhold the names or to ask that all or none be credited. There are occasions, too, when a photographer or artist whose specialization lies elsewhere prefers not to have his name identified with advertising. A third reason for the absence of an artist's or photographer's name is that no record of it exists.

In the world of advertising, everyone's thinking is focused on now or on the future, never on the past. Ask an agent or advertiser to recall, or to look up the names of the persons responsible for an ad created fifteen or twenty years ago, let alone fifty, and it's like talking to him of the Middle Ages. Because files cannot be kept forever, and because advertisers have often changed agents and personnel, too many gaps exist in earlier records for the agents to be credited with sufficient consistency throughout the hundred years this book covers. Instead, it must suffice to give thanks, heartfelt thanks—on page 319—collectively to the talents known to have been involved, and to any others who may, inadvertently, have been missed.

ADVERTISING

How and when advertising began is anyone's guess. But taking into account that human nature has changed little if at all in thousands of years, it seems reasonable to suppose that the born promoter has always been with us, the intuitive salesman with his finger on the public's pulse, the genius who, in singing for his supper, knows the precise note to hit hardest when putting a new idea, service, or product across.

Or is it that advertising has influenced our thinking for so long now that to imagine an astute merchant or politician of any day or age not blowing his own trumpet or hiring a clever talent to do it for him is virtually impossible? It is said that even the great Leonardo alerted the Sforzas to the propaganda value of his artistic activities, regarding himself as 'something between a genius and a public relations officer'.

Advertising is, of course, today's scene. No business can succeed without it, no name products appear on the market without being backed by advertising. Food, clothing, furniture, accessories, cosmetics, books, toys, everything displayed in the store is there as a result of intensive competition and expensive promotion on the part of each manufacturer to induce the stores to stock and stack his product.

Advertising greets us in the morning mail—and on the toothpaste tube. We eat and drink what's advertised, whether at breakfast, lunch, or dinner. We've even been sold the idea that it's 'in,' cool, or chic to wear shirts and pants with a trade name printed across the front or back—and nightwear, too, so we can go to bed hugging advertising.

For the most part we love it, secretly at least. We may resent the hideous sign that invades the beauty spot, loathe the commercial that interrupts a TV show, but we reach for our newspaper or favourite magazine not only for an update on the news but to scan the ads for bargains or to enjoy looking at all those

beautiful people showing us all those beautiful things to buy, see, or do.

Relaxed and snug in our push-button homes, thumbing through the luxury magazines—or a glamorous catalogue artfully designed to arrive before Christmas—we find ourselves dazzled not by the fruits of man's ingenuity and work alone, but by the attractive manner in which all these objects are spread before us. Everything we might need and everything we could manage without but might be tempted to buy just the same is within easy reach of the telephone and charge account.

Seldom does it cross anyone's mind, while disposing of these quality catalogues and magazines, what fortunes are invested in them. The cost of an average colour ad is comparable to the price tag on a major work of art along Bond Street or Madison Avenue. It's not just the cost of the space in the media—always high enough—but the photographer's fee, sometimes the cost of hiring models, going far on location, renting props, employing the service of an expert stylist or makeup artist. To these considerations must be added the copywriter, the designer or art director, and the type and very expensive four-colour separations. All this, incidentally, for the artwork to be consigned to limbo after the campaign is over unless the artist has arranged to get back more than a proof of his ad.

Advertising has had a long and vivid history, but what we see of it today is almost entirely the outgrowth of the late Victorian age. Traces of this oldest form of disposable art prior to the beginning of the nineteenth century are extremely few and far between.

Sometimes the prehistoric cave painter is pointed to as the father of the poster artist because of the simple and direct manner in which he too communicated messages from the surface of a wall. One of the earliest actual evidences of advertis-

6

ing is an inscription in the form of propaganda found on a 3000 B.C. Egyptian tomb. Twenty-five hundred or more years later, theatre-loving Athenians were distributing engraved announcements of their plays. The ancient Greeks also evolved a square rotating column on which to post important notices and proclamations. Possibly, too, they painted ads on walls, to be copied later characteristically by the Romans, who publicized their gladiatorial combats in this fashion.

Handsome restored examples, or copies, exist of the work of the medieval commercial artist, the itinerant who journeyed through villages and towns painting signs like those that customarily hang outside country inns and sometimes still ornament tradesmen's shops, such as those of the apothecary, pawnbroker, tailor, and barber. To contemporary eyes these antiquities seem purely decorative, but their original purpose was practical: to inform the illiterate where to go for this or that service.

History was made in 1477 when William Caxton pulled from his handpress the first ad to be printed in the English language. The announcement, beautifully done but in content considerably less momentous than the event itself, made known that 'pyes [service books] of Salisburi use' were available 'good Chepe' at the sign of the Red Pale in the Almonry at Westminster.

In time, tradesmen were ordering printed announcements in the form of bills or cards for exhibition purposes or to hand out to the passersby. At first these ads were straight type designs, later becoming much fancier, with Roman script and flowing characters. Printed playbills became increasingly common from the sixteenth century onward. These bills were distributed by hand until someone suddenly awoke to the bright idea of pasting them on the posts that lined the streets—hence the word 'poster'. But it was not until after Charles Dickens used it in his 1838 novel *Nicholas Nickleby* that 'poster' finally made the English dictionary. By that time the posts that had protected pedestrians from traffic had been replaced by pavements with curbs. And so the poster was to find a new home—pasted on a signboard or directly on a wall.

When Londoners opened the first number of *The Times* on January 1, 1788, they would have been surprised to find two shipping advertisements, each illustrated with a small line drawing. Today these are regarded as the ancestor of the illustrated advertisement. But almost another hundred years were to pass before the concept of press and magazine advertising changed radically with the perfecting of the photoengraving or halftone process. Until then illustrations for printed ads had to be rendered in line and reproduced by means of a hand-carved woodblock or metal engraving. With photoengraving, any painting, drawing, or photograph could be photographed and etched with acid in continuous tone from dark to light directly onto the printing plate itself, in any size required. The printed result came

Advertisement by William Caxton. 1477 (Bodleian Library)

as close to the original artwork as we have grown accustomed to find in reproductions today.

Meanwhile, the power press, invented in 1810, had replaced the hand-operated press, and by the 1850s was sufficiently advanced for sheets to be printed at the rate of approximately 10,000 an hour on a small press, and proportionately fewer on a larger one. Thus not only had the Industrial Revolution introduced the machinery whereby everyday objects could be produced en masse, but the media through which they could be sold en masse.

It paid to advertise. Not that all customers were such a pushover as the little Victorian lady who, dying to try out the new patent medicine she had just purchased, exclaimed to her friend, "My dear, it *must* be good because the advertisement spoke so *very* highly of it." Nevertheless, business boomed, more and more companies advertised, and the Victorians prospered.

From the journals of the day we see that the richer the Victorians became in the latter half of the century, the fussier were their clothes, the more gingerbready their architecture, the more overstuffed their houses. Inevitably the fad for clutter reached the ad columns, and it could almost be said that the bolder and heavier the printers' typefaces became, the more extravagant the advertisers' claims. By the 1880s, cures for everything were advertised, from cholera to dyspepsia, from pimples to torpid livers; there were health belts and tummy shrinkers, elixirs to restore youth to the aging and tonics to make hair grow, soften, curl, glisten, or—to judge from some of the illustrations—stand on end. Aesthetics took second place to the message. No advertiser was talking about art; he was talking about ads that paid.

Despite the trend, and although the Medici of the advertising world were yet to come, the nineteenth century produced Jules Chéret whose new experiments with colour lithography, based on Aloys Senefelder's 1798 invention, combined with his popular *joie de vivre* style, led to the birth of the golden age of the poster—the point at which this visual history of advertising begins.

1880-1900

In 1880 Victoria, now sixty-one, was still queen of a prosperous England, her far-flung empire defended by a navy that made her the mistress of the seas.

That year in America James Abram Garfield, the last President of the United States to be born in a log cabin, also became one of the shortest-lived occupants of the White House. Barely sixteen years had passed since the Lincoln tragedy when, on July 2, 1881, Garfield, returning home to his invalid wife, was shot by an assassin claiming to have been 'inspired by God'. When Garfield died on September nineteenth, Chester Alan Arthur became the twenty-first President of the United States.

The Industrial Revolution, the force behind the nineteenth century's unprecedented productivity, had made the world smaller with the invention of the steam locomotive and the development of railroads. Garfield, a Congressman in 1873, praised the railway as 'the greatest centralizing force in modern times'. A good example of this was the Central and Union Pacific railroads, then proudly advertising a service that brought San Francisco and New York—separated by three thousand miles of rugged territory—'only six days and twenty hours' apart. This first transcontinental rail route, the world's longest, cost the first-class passenger a hundred and forty dollars, the 'emigrant' seventy-five.

By 1880 the telephone, phonograph, and electric light bulb had been invented. The first electric light sign appeared on Broadway in 1891, and within two years the avenue was 'The Great White Way'. In 1885 Karl Benz and Gottlieb Daimler were producing the ancestors of today's automobile, the Lumière brothers were showing the first moving picture in 1895, and the following year Guglielmo Marconi patented his wireless telegraphy system in England.

While long journeys might be undertaken by train or steamship in the 1880s, local mobility depended on the feet, the horse, or, just possibly, the bicycle. The age of the two-wheeler had barely begun, but in 1896, when Will Owen was designing his famous posters for Victor (page 24), it was in full spin.

Entertainment was concentrated mostly around the home. The new craze, lawn tennis, was getting to be as popular as croquet, and party games were played as illustrated in Kate Greenaway's *Book of Games*—the queen of the nursery's picture book of 1889. More practical pastimes were sewing, knitting, carpentry, painting, and photography—especially after George

Eastman's hand-held box camera came on the market in 1888 (page 13). Taken together, hobbies amounted to big business. Even letter-writing, an art in Victorian days, used tons of notepaper, collectors of stamps and postcards used quantities of albums, and the piano, the focal point of the 'withdrawing-room', where the family sang, danced, and otherwise entertained, was also the sheet music publisher's greatest delight.

New periodicals, including *The Ladies' Home Journal* and the original *Life,* a magazine of humour, both originating in 1883, kept springing up, and it was common for a novel first to be serialized in a magazine, then issued in book form later on. An older generation, brought up on Dickens, Hawthorne, Melville, and Poe, now read the younger novelists, such as Thomas Hardy, Henry James, Mark Twain, Rudyard Kipling, and Conan Doyle.

In the provinces few entertainments were looked forward to with such eagerness as the circus. The excitement began directly the bright Strobridge lithos were posted announcing the newest and 'greatest show on earth' (page 38). In 1883 Buffalo Bill joined the competition with his Wild West spectacles. Road companies offered variety or vaudeville shows, burlesque, comedy, or the all-out farce, like Brandon Thomas's ever-popular *Charley's Aunt.* The full-blooded melodrama could also pack the house; the success of one of these hero-heroine-villain shows usually being judged backstage not so much by the bravos and whistles the hero and the heroine received as by the loudness of the hisses, boos, and catcalls aimed at the villain.

A night out in the big city might mean seeing a play with Henry Irving or Ellen Terry in the lead, Ada Rehan, the Duse, or the 'divine Sarah' (page 14). Music lovers might go to hear Bizet, Gounod, Verdi, Wagner, or perhaps a rollicking Gilbert and Sullivan at D'Oyly Carte's new Savoy (page 21). Queen Victoria, an avid theatre-goer, loved to flit from play to play, sampling bits of several hits in a single evening.

In the 1890s two great Irish-born playwrights, George Bernard Shaw, a key figure in the Fabian Society, and Oscar Wilde, England's leading aesthete, whose affectations were parodied by Gilbert and Sullivan in *Patience,* were headline news. Shaw's first play, *Widowers' Houses,* a *succès de scandale* in 1892, was followed by *Mrs. Warren's Profession,* which, dealing candidly with the oldest profession, was automatically banned in England and, when it opened in America, caused the actress in the role of

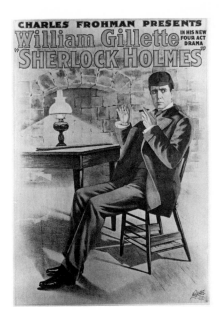

Mrs. Warren to be arrested on charges of disorderly conduct. English audiences finally got to see Mrs. Warren in 1925.

Shaw went on to new heights, but Wilde's triumphs were short-lived. His first play, *Lady Windermere's Fan*, written for Lillie Langtry in 1892, was a success; his last, *The Importance of Being Earnest*, described as the 'most brilliantly amusing farce in the language', was the stage sensation of 1895. So, offstage, was Wilde's affair with Lord Alfred Douglas, which had suddenly burst into the open, causing Wilde's downfall, imprisonment, ruin, and, indirectly, his death five years later in Paris at the age of forty-six.

Front-page news of a very different kind revolved about the Millais-Pears affair. In 1886 Sir William Ingram bought John Everett Millais' portrait of his young grandson, William James—later to become a stern and bearded admiral—blowing bubbles (page 10)—with the object of reproducing the painting in his *Illustrated London News*. Sir William then sold the painting to Thomas J. Barratt, the manager of Pears, who saw what a wonderful poster it would make with a cake of soap added at the bottom. To the academic world this was a sacrilege, but the public so loved 'Bubbles' that the poster made advertising history as the sales of soap soared. John Guille Millais wrote perceptively in the biography of his father: 'We ought to be grateful to them [Pears] for their spirited departure from the track of advertisers. The example that they set has tended to raise the character of our illustrated advertisements, whether in papers or posters, and may possibly lead to the final extinction of such atrocious vulgarities as now offend the eye at every turn.'

Pears was the first English company to realize the immense possibilities of prestige advertising, but Paris had been flowering her city walls with lithographic masterpieces for years.

As opposed to the man's world of London, Paris was the centre of feminine fashions, indeed of femininity itself. Parisian night life of the *belle époque* was epitomized by the most famous of all nightclubs, the Moulin Rouge, and by the Folies-Bergère, both of which put on the gayest and naughtiest of revues with the greatest style. In keeping with the effervescent spirit of Paris were Jules Chéret's sparkling posters of pretty girls—'Chérettes' they were called—smiling, skating, dancing, or otherwise engaged (pages 18-19). A contemporary critic, Karl Huysman, wrote in 1880 that in his opinion there was 'a thousand times more talent in the smallest of Chéret's posters than in the majority of pictures on the walls of the Paris Salon.' This was as much a comment on the Salon as on Chéret, and must have

pleased the impressionists, led by Monet, Pissarro, Renoir, and Manet, who themselves had so long been ignored by the Salon. A modern photographic interpretation by Steve Campbell of Manet's superb 'Bar at the Folies-Bergère', painted in 1881, appears in the Campari ad on page 318.

In Paris the response to Chéret influenced advertisers to engage other 'serious' artists to design posters, among them Alphonse Mucha (page 14), recently arrived from Austria, Swiss-born Théophile Alexandre Steinlen (page 25), Pierre Bonnard, and Henri de Toulouse-Lautrec (page 17). Lautrec's posters, the last designed in 1891, were not nearly so popular as Chéret's. The earthier models, flat surfaces, strong outlines, and shadowless techniques of his lithographs—much influenced by Japanese prints and now so valued—were not pretty enough then for the public's taste.

The golden age of the poster reached its height about 1895. At that time England's distinguished designers included the Beggarstaffs, as the brothers-in-law James Pryde and William Nicholson were called (page 16), Dudley Hardy (page 21), Maurice Grieffenhagen, and Aubrey Beardsley (page 20), the twenty-two-year-old genius discovered by *The Studio* and featured in the magazine's first issue in 1893.

The year 1893 was also that of Chicago's Columbian Exposition, and the year too that Anton Dvorak composed his *From the New World* symphony. Posters had become the rage in America, and the enterprise of new magazines like *Century*, *Harper's*, *Lippincott*, and *The Chap-Book* encouraged the talents of Will Bradley and Maxfield Parrish, both influenced by Beardsley, also those of Edward Penfield and Ethel Reed—all represented in the illustrations that follow.

FROM LEFT TO RIGHT:

Queen Victoria. From a photograph taken in 1872

Gilbert and Sullivan's *Pirates of Penzance*. The original programme 1880

Lillie Langtry in a poster for Pears' soap. 1890's

Psyche. The original White Rock mineral water ad, painted by Paul Thuman in 1893

Edward, Prince of Wales (later King Edward VII) with the Duke of York. 1892

Poster for a play based on Conan Doyle's Sherlock Holmes stories. 1899

Pears' shaving soap. Ad. 1891. A & F Pears Ltd

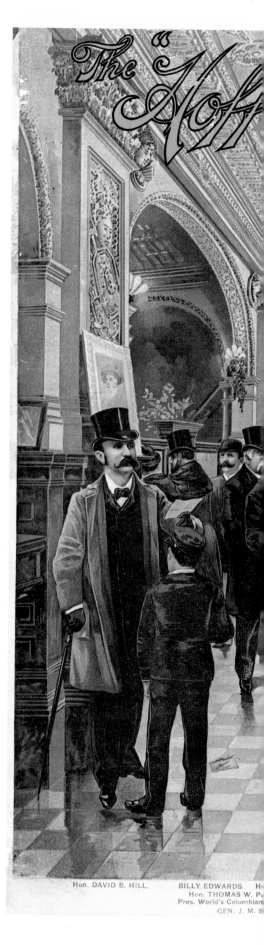

'Bubbles'. Painting used in advertising Pears' soap.
John Everett Millais. 1886. A & F Pears Ltd

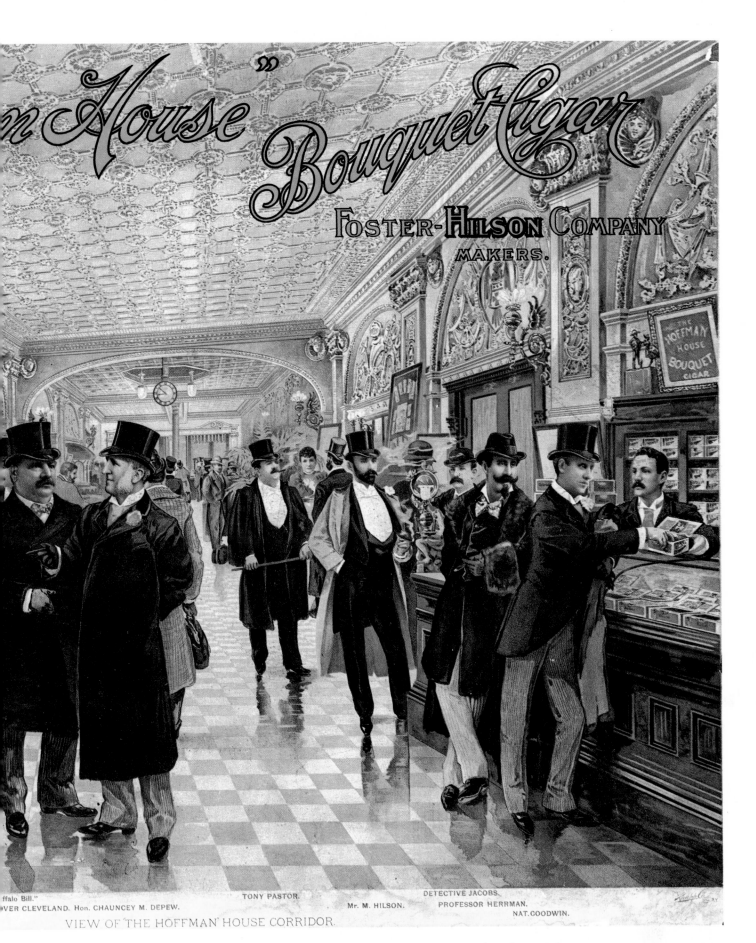

The 'Hoffman House' Bouquet Cigar. Ad. c. 1893. Foster-Hilson Company

THE ILLUSTRATED LONDON NEWS

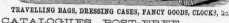

MAPPIN & WEBB

Supply the public direct from their London Warehouses at

WHOLESALE PRICES.

ELECTRO-SILVER PLATE. Highest obtainable Quality.

STERLING SILVER Novelties for presents.

SPOONS & FORKS. 20 years' Wear guaranteed.

TABLE KNIVES. (M. & W.'s Patent.)

TRAVELLING BAGS, DRESSING CASES, FANCY GOODS, CLOCKS, &c.

ILLUSTRATED CATALOGUES POST-FREE.

No. 1. Plate and Table Knives. No. 2. Travelling Bags and Cases. No. 3. Sporting Knives, Razors, Scissors, &c.

MAPPIN & WEBB, MANSION HOUSE BUILDINGS, CITY; AND OXFORD-ST., W.: LONDON.

MANUFACTORY—The Royal Cutlery and Plate Works, SHEFFIELD.

BY SPECIAL ROYAL APPOINTMENT.

Spearman's

No other article woven equals this in general utility.

PURE WOOL ONLY! **DEVON**

According to the "Queen." "It has no rival."

SERGES

For Ladies' wear, beautiful qualities, 1s. 6d. to 4s. 6d. the yard; for Children's wear, capitally strong, 1s. 3d. to 2s. the yard; for Gentlemen's wear, double width, 3s. 6d. to 10s. 6d. the yard. The Navy Blues and the Blacks are fast dyes. On receipt of instructions, samples will be sent Post-Free.—N.B. Any length cut, and Carriage Paid to principal Railway Stations.

Only Address: SPEARMAN and SPEARMAN, Plymouth. NO AGENTS.

Accommodates 500 Guests.

THE LANGHAM

PORTLAND-PLACE, W.

This cosmopolitan HOTEL has been thoroughly redecorated, and combines every improvement and luxury. Sumptuous Apartments for Private Dinners and Wedding Breakfasts. Recherché Table-d'hôte (open to non-residents) from 6.30 to 8 p.m.

Price 2.6 each.

THE "PARKER" UMBRELLA REGISTERED.

5000 SILK UMBRELLAS,

2s. 6d. each, direct from the Manufacturer. Ladies' or Gents' Plain or Twill Silk, Paragon frames, beautifully carved and mounted sticks, sent Parcels Post-free, 2s. 9d. (or 36 stamps). 15,000 sold in twelve months. List and testimonials free. Re-covering, &c., neatly done.

Address,

J. E. PARKER,

Umbrella Works, Broom-close, Sheffield.

ELLIMAN'S ROYAL EMBROCATION.

"Castle Weir, Kington, Herefordshire, "December, 1878.

"Gentlemen,—I use the Royal Embrocation in the stables and kennels, and have found it very serviceable. I have also used the Universal Embrocation for lumbago and rheumatism for the last two years, and have suffered very little since using it." "R. H. PRICE, Lieut.-Col., Master of Radnorshire Hunt."

From Captain S. G. Button, J.P., St. Brendon's, Clonfert, Eyrecourt, county Galway. "Dec. 16, 1884.

"Sirs,—Elliman's Royal Embrocation is in use in my stables, and I find the results most satisfactory.

"Master of the Kilkenny Foxhounds."

Of Chemists and Saddlers, in Bottles, 2s., 2s. 6d., and 3s. 6d. Proprietors, ELLIMAN, SONS, and CO., Slough.

GOLDSMITHS' ALLIANCE

(LIMITED),

LATE A. B. SAVORY AND SONS,

SILVER AND BEST SILVER-PLATED MANUFACTURERS,

11 & 12, CORNHILL, LONDON, E.C.

(Opposite the Bank of England.)

SPOONS & FORKS.

TEA & COFFEE SERVICES.

WAITERS & TRAYS.

CLARET JUGS & GOBLETS.

CRUET & BREAKFAST FRAMES.

INKSTANDS, CANDLESTICKS.

ALCESTER.

Massive Silver Bowl, richly chased, gilt inside, on ebonized plinth, to hold 9 pints ... £20 0 0 Larger size, ditto, 13 pints 25 10 0

A new Pamphlet of Prices, Illustrated with over 500 Engravings, will be forwarded, gratis and post-free, on application.

THE "EASY" LAWN MOWER

Is now made with 5 Knives. All sizes from "10 to 30" kept in Stock.

TRADE MARK THE "EASY" LAWN MOWER

30 INCH EASY

UNSOLICITED TESTIMONIAL

FROM The Steward of the Earl of Shrewsbury.

"Alton Towers. "May 20, 188".

"Your Machines are first-class. I find them an immense saving of labour.

Apply for List to any Ironmonger or Seedsman, or direct to the Sole Licensees.

SELIG, SONNENTHAL & CO., 85, QUEEN VICTORIA-STREET, LONDON, E.C.

JOHN WARD 246 & 247, TOTTENHAM-COURT-ROAD

(LATE OF SAVILLE HOUSE, LEICESTER-SQUARE), LONDON.

INVALID CHAIR MANUFACTURER TO THE QUEEN AND ROYAL FAMILY.

The largest assortment in the world of INVALID CHAIRS, SPINAL COUCHES, BATH CHAIRS, BED TABLES, and INVALID FURNITURE, &c., for Sale or Hire.

Prize Medals—London, 1851 and 1862; Paris, 1855, 1867, and 1878 (3 Medals); Vienna, 1873 (2 Medals); Dublin, 1865.

Established 150 years.

Price Catalogues Post-free.

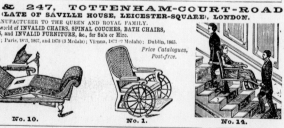

No. 19. No. 10. No. 1. No. 14.

FAULKNER'S CELEBRATED DIAMONDS. SPANISH CRYSTALS.

DETECTION IMPOSSIBLE.

KNOWN all over the **WORLD** as the **FINEST STONES** ever Produced.

21s. BUMBLE BEE BROOCH. CAT'S-EYE HEAD, RUBY EYES. 27s. 21s.

GNAT BROOCH, 12s. 6d. Larger, 16s. 6d.

Price 16s. 6d. SPRAY BROOCH, 30s.

Price 62s.

SCARF PIN, 12s. Smaller, 10s. 12s. CASE, 1s. 6d.

SHIRT STUD, to match, in Gold, 2s., 10s.

SCREW EARRINGS, 20s., 25s. Smaller, 10s., 12s. Ditto with Wires, at same Price.

There Magnificent Stones are set in GOLD, HALL-MARKED, and made by most experienced workmen; detection impossible; and I defy the BEST JUDGES to tell them from DIAMONDS. The brilliancy and lustre are most marvellous, and equal to BRILLIANTS.

WORTH TWENTY GUINEAS.

The Stones being real Crystals, and splendidly faceted. They will resist acids, alkalies, and intense heat. All stones set by diamond-setters, and beautifully finished.

Single-stone Earrings, from 10s. per pair; Scarf Pins, shirt Studs, Pendants, Necklets, &c., 30s. to £20. Much worn for Court and other occasions. Testimonials from all parts of the World. These stones are daily gaining great reputation throughout the World, and have been awarded Three Prize Medals from the Great Exhibitions.

The Public are earnestly invited to INSPECT our marvellous selection now ON VIEW, which astonishes all Visitors. Catalogues post-free.

NOTICE.—These stones cannot possibly be had elsewhere, and are only to be obtained of the SOLE IMPORTER and MANUFACTURER.

ARTHUR O. FAULKNER, 174, High-street, Notting-hill-gate, London, W. Established 1860.

NEW PREMISES ALSO AT 203, REGENT-ST., W.

ESTABLD MOUSON & CO'S 1798

FIRST PRIZE MED. REGISTD TRADE MARK LONDON, VIENNA, SYDNEY &c.

CELEBRATED TOILET SOAPS

MOUSON and CO.'S Toilet Soaps are warranted to be made of the very best and purest materials, not to shrink or vary in shape or weight, even if kept for years.

Improved Toilet Soaps assorted in Honey, Rose, and Windsor.

Cocoa Butter Soap, a veritable medicinal soap for softening the skin.

Spring Violet Soap, of the natural perfume, pronounced, even by rival makers, unequalled.

Aromatic Vegetable Soap, a bijou for the Nursery, pure and uncoloured, with a splendid perfume of hers.

Handy and Handsome (Registered Mark), a new and most conveniently shaped Toilet Soap.

"The Challenge" Windsor Soap (Regd. Mark), wonderfully mild and of excellent perfume.

J. G. MOUSON and CO., Perfumers, FRANKFORT-ON-MAIN; and 32 and 33, HAMSELL-STREET, LONDON, E.C.

To be had of the principal Wholesale Perfumers and Druggists throughout the Country.

EXTRA QUALITY

DUNLAP & CO

COPYRIGHTED

FALL STYLES

NOW ON SALE

at our own stores and authorized agents throughout the
United States.

Blair's Pills
Great English Remedy for
GOUT and RHEUMATISM.
SAFE, SURE, EFFECTIVE.
Druggists, or 224 William St., New York.

DON'T BOIL Whitman's INSTANTANEOUS
Chocolate—doesn't need it
Made in a jiffy, with
boiling water or milk. Sold everywhere.

"BARKER
BRAND"
COLLARS
ARE
THE
BEST.
Linen Both Sides
Wm BARKER, Manufacturer. TROY, N.Y.

OPIUM HABIT AND **DRUNKENNESS**
Cured in 10 to 20 Days. No Pay till
Cured. DR. J.L. STEPHENS, LEBANON, OHIO.

TAKEN WITH A PHOTAKE

EXACT SIZE OF PICTURE

THE PHOTAKE
with Complete Outfit **CAMERA**
for taking and developing
Six Negatives and print-
ing Twelve Pictures. **$2.50**
Prepaid to any part of the U. S. for

Takes Five Pictures on glass plates at one loading
(no kink—films to handle). Makes it easy to develop and finish
pictures, which is half the pleasure of amateur photography, at
minimum cost. Takes any kind of picture, Snap Shot,
Flash Light, or Time Exposure. Has Long Focus, and
will not distort. Made of seamless metal, handsomely finished.
Simplest of all to operate. Gives best results. Every one
tested and guaranteed. Send 2c. stamps for booklet and sample
picture. Chicago Camera Co., Room 31 Garden City Blk. Chicago.

EARL & WILSON'S.
MEN'S LINEN COLLARS AND CUFFS
"ARE THE BEST"
FOR SALE EVERYWHERE.

BLOOD POISON
A SPECIALTY Primary, Secondary or Ter-
tiary BLOOD POISON permanently
cured in 15 to 35 days. You can be treated at
home for same price under same guaranty. If you prefer to come here we will con-
tract to pay railroad fare and hotel bills, and
no charge, if we fail to cure. If you have taken mer-
cury, iodide potash, and still have aches and
pains, Mucous Patches in mouth, Sore Throat,
Pimples, Copper Colored Spots, Ulcers on
any part of the body, Hair or Eyebrows falling
out, it is this Secondary BLOOD POISON
we guarantee to cure. We solicit the most obsti-
nate cases and challenge the world for a
case we cannot cure. This disease has always
baffled the skill of the most eminent physi-
cians. $500,000 capital behind our uncondi-
tional guaranty. Absolute proofs sent sealed on
application. Address COOK REMEDY CO.,
307 Masonic Temple, CHICAGO, ILL.

HENRY LINDENMEYR & SONS,
PAPER WAREHOUSE.
Nos. 21, 23, 35 and 37 East Houston Street, Puck Building,
Branch Warehouse, 20 Beekman Street, NEW YORK.
ALL KINDS OF PAPER MADE TO ORDER.

CAMPAIGN Badges, Banners, Flags, Everything,
Clubs, Merchants, Agents supplied.
Wholesale price list and sample but
on mailed for stamp. GRISWOLD & CO., 108 Fulton St., N.Y.

WANTED—AN IDEA Who can think of
some simple thing
to patent? Protect
your ideas; they may bring you wealth. Write
JOHN WEDDERBURN & CO., Patent Attorneys,
Washington, D. C., for their $1800 prize offer and list of
200 inventions wanted.

Photography
Simplified.

Picture
taking
with the
Improved
Bullet
camera is
the refine-
ment of
photo-
graphic
luxury.
It makes
photog-
raphy easy
for the novice—delightful for everybody.

LOADS IN DAYLIGHT with
our light-proof film cartridges, or can be
used with glass plates. Splendid achromatic
lens, improved rotary shutter, set of three
stops. Handsome finish.

Price, Improved No. 2 Bullet, for pictures 3½ x 3½
inches, $10.00
Light-proof Film Cartridge, 12 exposures, 3½ x 3½ .60

EASTMAN KODAK CO.
Booklet Free. Rochester, N.Y.

The Hoffman House Cigar

ABSOLUTELY UNEQUALED

Hoffman
House
BOUQUET
CIGAR

THE HILSON CO
MAKERS
NEW YORK

"HAS STOOD THE TEST FOR YEARS"

If your Dealer does not keep them,
Order DIRECT from us.

This IS THE 1896
SEARCH LIGHT
PRICE $5.00

The only strictly first
class bicycle lantern on
the market.

Ask your dealer or send to

BRIDGEPORT BRASS CO.

Or
19 Murray Street, New York,
85-87 Pearl Street, Boston,
17 No. 7th St., Philadelphia.
Bridgeport,
Conn.

Send for Catalogue No. 48

Buy $1.00 worth Dobbins's Floating-Borax
Soap of your grocer; send wrappers to Dob-
bins Soap Manufacturing Company, Philadelphia Pa. They will send you free of charge,
postage paid, a Worcester Pocket Dictionary,
298 pages bound in cloth profusely illustrated.
Offer good until August 1st only.

"Hear dem bells a ringing,
dey's ringing everywhere."

THEY HAVE A TONE THATS ALL THEIR OWN.

ELEGANT BOOKLET FREE ON APPLICATION

The Chimes of Normandy could
not excel in sweetness and purity of tone

THE
New Departure
BICYCLE BELLS

The standard of excellence the
wide world over. In 16 different styles and prices. All deal
ers sell them.

The New Departure Bell Co., Bristol, Conn., U.S.A.

" What's this I hear about the plumber and
the paper-hanger in the next square? Have
they been exchanging houses?" "Not exactly. They did a lot of work for each other,
and each had to take the other's house for his
pay." —Tid-Bits.

M. Stachelberg & Co's Havana Cigars
EST. 1857.
COSTLIEST BECAUSE BEST

Rae's Lucca Oil
The Perfection of Olive Oil

Your physician will tell you that Olive
Oil, pure and sweet, is one of the most
wholesome of foods. Rae's Oil is pure and
sweet, as testified to by numerous awards
and wide repute. A trial will convince
you of its superior excellence as a food
product.

Guaranteed Absolutely Pure by

S. RAE & CO.,
Established 1836. Leghorn, Italy.

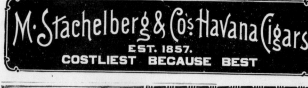

See the wonderful Statue Cartoons in

LESLIE'S WEEKLY.

They are the hit of the campaign. The
above is a reduced specimen.

LESLIE'S WEEKLY

is doing valiant work for sound money and
protection. Send a dollar for a three-
months' trial trip.

ARKELL WEEKLY CO.,
110 Fifth Avenue, New York.

GREAT AMERICA'S GREATEST CHAMPAGNE: "GREAT WESTERN."
"GREAT WESTERN"

in 1895 reached the
5TH PLACE
in the sale of Cham-
pagne in the UNITED STATES.
MUST BE A REASON FOR THIS.
PLEASANT VALLEY WINE COMPANY, Cellars: RHEIMS, STEUBEN CO., NEW YORK.

"GREAT WESTERN"
is now used in many
of the best Hotels,
Clubs and Homes in
preference to For-
eign Vintages.

For sale by all first-class
Grocers & Wine Merchants.

Southwestern Limited — BEST TRAIN FOR CINCINNATI AND ST. LOUIS. — Daily by the New York Central.

Advertisements in *Judge.* September 12, 1896. The Judge Publishing Co

Advertisements in *The Illustrated London News.* March 21, 1885. *The Illustrated London News*

Lorenzaccio (Sarah Bernhardt). Poster. Alphonse Mucha. 1896.
Théâtre de la Renaissance, Paris

Planet and Neptune tobaccos. Ad. 1895. Buchanan & Lyall Tobacco Co

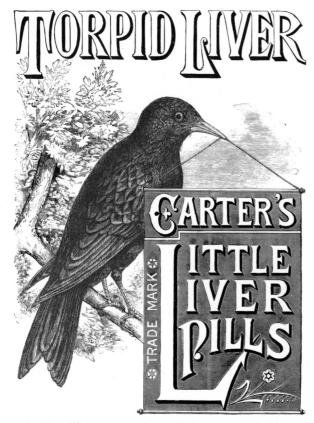

Carter's Little Liver Pills. Ad. 1890. Carters Ltd

Rowntree's Elect Cocoa. Poster. The Beggarstaffs
(James Pryde and William Nicholson.) 1894.
Rowntree & Co., Ltd

The Echo: Chicago's new paper. Will H. Bradley. 1895.
The Echo, Chicago

OPPOSITE:
Babylone d'Allemagne, book by Victor Joze. Poster.
Henri de Toulouse-Lautrec. 1894.
Imprimerie Chaix

Duke Cigarettes are the Best. Card. c. 1888.
The Duke Tobacco Company

'Fête d'Artistes'. Poster. Jules Chéret. 1885.
Musée Grévin

La Loïe Fuller. Poster. Jules Chéret. 1893.
Folies-Bergère, Paris

Leona Dare. Poster. Jules Chéret. 1890. Imprimerie Chaix

ISOLDE

'Isolde'. Poster for Oscar Wilde's play poem. Aubrey Beardsley. 1895. *The Studio*

The Chieftain, operetta. Poster. Dudley Hardy. 1896. The D'Oyly Carte Opera Company

THE CHIEFTAIN

BY
F. C. BURNAND
&
ARTHUR
SULLIVAN.

Dudley Hardy

SAVOY THEATRE.

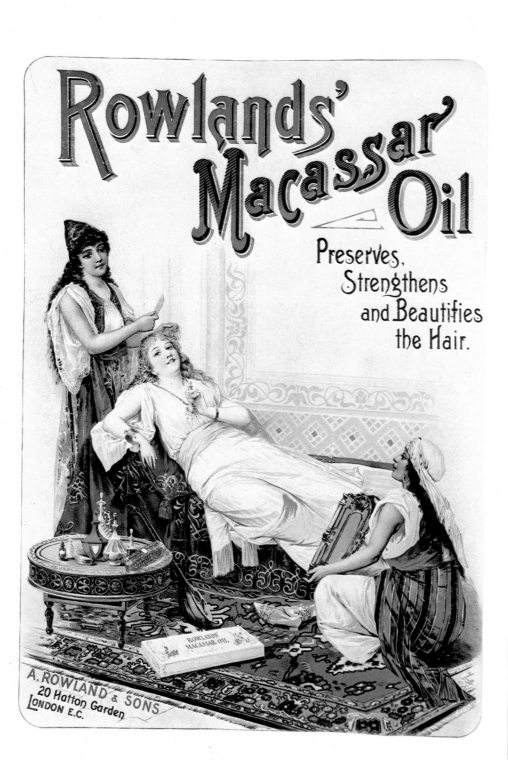

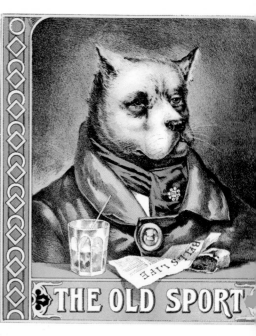

OPPOSITE LEFT:
Rowland's Macassar Oil. Ad. c. 1895. A. Rowland & Sons

OPPOSITE BOTTOM:
'The Old Sport' plug tobacco. Display card. 1880s

ABOVE:
Batty & Co's 'The' Sauce. Ad. 1890s. Batty & Co

RIGHT:
Horniman's Tea. Display card. 1890s. Lyons Tetley

A Pre-Raphaelite Collection. Poster. W. Graham Robertson.
1890s. The Goupil Gallery

BELOW:
'Arabella and Araminta' stories by Gertrude Smith.
Poster (detail). Ethel Reed. 1895. Copeland and Day, Boston

BOTTOM:
Victor Bicycles. Poster. Will H. Bradley. 1896.
Overman Wheel Co

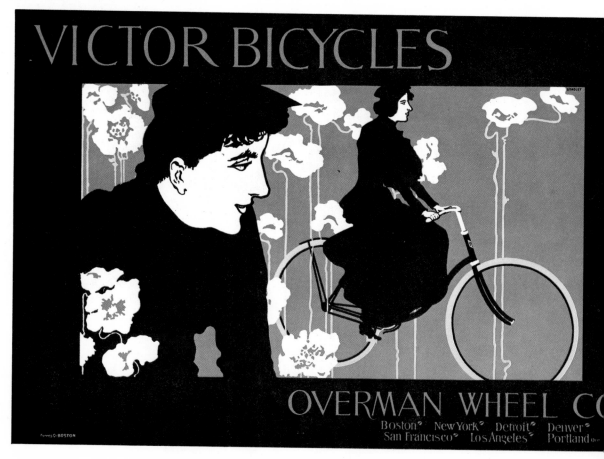

HE ADLAKE CAMERA

x 5", with **twelve** plate holders , **$12.**

ABOVE:
The Adlake Camera. Poster. Maxfield Parrish. 1897.
The Adlake Camera Co

BELOW:
Motocycles Comiot. Poster. Théophile Alexandre Steinlen.
1899. Motocycles Comiot, Paris

RIGHT:
Harper's magazine. Cover. Edward Penfield. 1897.

Bird's Custard Powder: 'Kitchen Warfare'. Poster. M. Brodie. 1896. A. Bird & Sons, Ltd

Colman's Starch. Ad. 1890s. J. & J. Colman Ltd

Skipped by the Light of the Moon, musical comedy. Poster (detail). Dudley Hardy. 1900. Management: George Walton

Armour's Extract of Beef. Ad. 1899. Armour & Company

1900-1920

At the turn of the century there was a marked difference between the mood of the Old World and the New.

The United States, with its vast stretches of unoccupied territory, was indeed the Promised Land. The exciting Oklahoma land rush days vividly described in Edna Ferber's novel *Cimarron* were as recent as 1889. In 1900 some 450,000 immigrants came to seek American citizenship—and by 1910 the number had more than doubled. With almost limitless natural resources, increasing manpower and business know-how, with no income tax and the Treasury showing a surplus, the country's future had never looked rosier.

This feeling of general optimism was merely heightened in 1901 when Theodore Roosevelt, the country's youngest and most energetic President, strode into the White House promising everyone a 'square deal'.

In contrast, England's mood was cautious, even apprehensive. Maintaining an Empire had its physical, financial, and moral problems. In 1901 Queen Victoria, revered image of an age that bore her name, died, and with her went the sense of security her people had enjoyed for more than sixty years. The unpopular Boer War (1899–1902) was the cause of internal bitterness and hostility towards Britain abroad. There was unrest in Ireland and trouble at home, not only over workers' demands for better pay and living conditions, which the Labour Party, just formed in 1900, championed, but over the increasingly militant suffragettes.

There was a rumour that Germany was studying plans for an invasion of England. No one really believed it, yet in 1903 when the Wright Brothers proved at Kitty Hawk that men could fly, and within six years Blériot succeeded in flying across the English Channel in twenty-six minutes, England's cheers changed to shocked silence as she realized the significance of what had happened. If Blériot could hop across England's 'moat', which, coupled with the navy, had been the country's infallible defence against European aggression, so could the Germans or anyone else.

By now, another wonder, the 'horseless carriage', had become the toy of the rich. While proud owners were having the time of their lives, others who still preferred horses to horsepower—and couldn't afford not to—resented being coated with dust every time a 'wretched' car went hooting and bumping past. But nothing could prevent the inevitable, and in 1908 when Henry Ford introduced his Model T, the first mass-produced car, a new age of motoring began.

Despite disturbing undercurrents of 'progress', the Edwardians, led by the most pleasure-loving of monarchs—Edward VII adored pretty faces and lobsters for tea—were as good at playing ostrich as the ladies were at feathering their hats. They sat down to six-course dinners, dressed to the nines for Ascot, watched a little tennis at Wimbledon and cricket at Lord's, played the new game of Ping-Pong, and fled to the Riviera at chilblain time. American millionaires, before opening their seaside 'cottages' at Newport, Bar Harbor, or Southampton, might take the Grand Tour of Europe, stopping en route in England to choose, perhaps, a Rolls-Royce (page 61) or to marry a title.

In 1910 King Edward died, and George V succeeded. Two American men of letters died that year also, Mark Twain and O. Henry. H. G. Wells, very much alive, came out with two new books, Edith Wharton finished *Ethan Frome,* and John Galsworthy's play, *Justice,* was produced.

In New York Caruso (page 87) sang at the Metropolitan in Puccini's new opera *Girl of the Golden West.* Broadway also had a new Victor Herbert hit, *Naughty Marietta,* a new clown, Fanny Brice, in *The Ziegfeld Follies of 1910,* and a slightly older clown, Marie Dressler, singing 'Heaven Will Protect the Working Girl' in *Tillie's Nightmare.*

It was a good season, too, for those whose idols included Marie Tempest, John Drew, Minnie Maddern Fiske, Maude Adams, Otis Skinner, John Barrymore and his sister Ethel (page 52). In 1910 Mrs. Patrick Campbell (page 52) was onstage in *The Foolish Virgin,* but her greatest triumph was to come in 1914 as Eliza Doolittle in George Bernard Shaw's *Pygmalion.* That was the year Somerset Maugham finished writing his greatest novel, *Of Human Bondage.*

In 1912 the White Star Line's *Titanic* (page 49), the biggest, most glamorous 'floating hotel' ever known, struck an iceberg on her maiden voyage to New York and sank with the loss of fourteen hundred and ninety lives. Bernard Shaw, often consulted on matters of topical interest because he could be counted on for good newspaper copy, criticized the gross mismanagement of the captain and crew instead of praising their heroism. This caused great public dismay and aroused a furious Conan Doyle to call Shaw a sadist. No disaster had made such headlines since the San Francisco earthquake and fire of 1906.

Three of the century's greatest cultural developments occurred between 1910 and 1920. One was the Russian Ballet (page 51), organized by Diaghilev in 1909 in Paris, danced in London in 1911 with Thomas Beecham conducting the orchestra, and in New York five years later. Nothing like this had been seen before. It was not only the dancing of Nijinsky, Karsavina, and company, or the music of Stravinsky, Debussy, and Ravel, or the fantastic settings by Bakst, Goncharova, Picasso, and Chagall; it was the total kaleidoscopic effect of the three integrated marvels, an advantage so lacking, for instance, in the solo and sceneless performances of the great Anna Pavlova (page 53) after she left Diaghilev.

More universal was the influence of jazz, which came out of the South, New Orleans most famously, and developed into the well-known derivatives danced to from the days of Irving Berlin's *Alexander's Ragtime Band* in 1911, through the Harlem nightclub era of the twenties, to today.

The third big contribution to the arts was the motion picture, which in twelve years had developed from a flickering twelve-minute nickelodeon novelty, *The Great Train Robbery* of 1903, into the art form created by D. W. Griffith in his full-length *Birth of a Nation*. Aided by the popularity of Lillian Gish, Mary Pickford, Douglas Fairbanks, Charlie Chaplin, and others who deserted the stage for Hollywood, motion pictures were becoming the world's favourite form of entertainment.

In the fine arts, popular taste was meeting new challenges. French impressionist and post-impressionist painting, exhibited for the first time in London in 1905 and 1910 respectively, was not at all appreciated, and in the Armory Show of 1913 in New York when expressionism, futurism, fauvism and cubism were first seen, much of the public was outraged. Said one young man, aghast at Marcel Duchamp's abstract *Nude Descending a Staircase*, 'If that's the way women are going to look in the future, I'm off girls.' Gibson's (page 56) were more to the taste—so, even, was Whistler's *Mother*.

Industrialist Frank Pick, of the London Underground Railways, was farsighted enough to see the value of art in advertising, and before World War I was commissioning work by artists of the stature of Frank Brangwyn and Spencer Pryce. Among his discoveries was Montana-born Edward McKnight Kauffer, whose Underground posters became world famous in the twenties through the forties.

John Hassall's 'Skegness' (page 42) is typical of the jolly, infectious poster the English loved in the 1910s—and still do.

Tom Browne's 'Johnnie Walker' ad, used in adaptations ever since, first appeared in 1906. Leonetto Cappiello, Cecil Aldin, Tony Sarg, Hans Rudi Erdt, and Ludwig Hohlwein were other leading designers of the period. In America Palmer Cox, Maxfield Parrish, J. C. Leyendecker, and Coles Phillips were making brand names familiar household words. Examples by all the above artists appear in the following pages.

In 1914 when a Serbian nationalist murdered Archduke Franz Ferdinand, heir to the Austrian Empire, the curtain arose on one of the most terrible dramas in European history—the Great War.

To begin with, recruits were made up of volunteers, and poster artists such as Alfred Leete were called upon to switch from selling products with a smile to playing on human emotions (pages 58-59).

After three years of utter horror at the front, Great Britain and France were joined by the United States, bringing the tragedy to an end on November 11, 1918. Meanwhile, in 1917, the Bolsheviks murdered the Russian Czar and his family to put into practice the theory of communism.

FROM LEFT TO RIGHT:

Cover design for *The Ladies' Home Journal* by George Gibbs. 1901
Poster for J. M. Barrie's play, *Peter Pan*. 1905
Tom Browne's original sketch. 'Johnnie Walker.' 1906
Poster for Ford cars by Cuningham. 1912
Wartime poster by Frank Brangwyn for *The Daily Chronicle*. c. 1915
'To Horse, Workers!'. Communist poster of 1919

Fry's Chocolates. Ad. Harold Copping. c. 1901. J. S. Fry & Sons, Ltd

Cadbury's Cocoa. Ad. Cecil Aldin. 1900. Cadbury & Bros Ltd

Anti-free trade propaganda poster. 1906.
The Conservative Party

BELOW:
Waterman's Ideal Fountain Pen. Ad. 1904.
L. E. Waterman Co

"*After all, no ink like Carter's*"

he above is a reproduction of *Abbott Graves'* oil painting, "The Old Bookkeeper," executed for
HE CARTER'S INK CO. Boston. New York. Chicago.

'After all, no ink like Carter's'. Ad.
Abott Graves. © 1900. The Carter Ink Co

OPPOSITE:
"Snag-Proof" boots. Ad. Palmer Cox. © 1900.
Lambertville Rubber Co

Baker's cocoa. Ad. 1906. Walter Baker & Co., Ltd

THE
RIGHT
FLOUR

Surrounding the gluten and starch cells in the wheat berry there is a layer of almost pure white fibre.   It is called cellulose and is as indigestible as sawdust. The presence of cellulose in flour cannot be detected except by special test.   But it makes a difference in the moisture absorbing quality and so lessens the number of loaves to the sack. Some millers permit cellulose to go into their flour, but it is eliminated from GOLD MEDAL FLOUR by our special purifying process.

Washburn-Crosby's
GOLD MEDAL FLOUR

Gold Medal Flour. Ad. © 1906. Washburn-Crosby Co

Macfarlane, Lang & Co's Cakes and Biscuits. Display card. c. 1906. Macfarlane, Lang & Co

Coca-Cola beverage. Display card. 1905. The Coca-Cola Co

Solarine metal polish. Display card. c. 1900.
Solarine Co., Inc

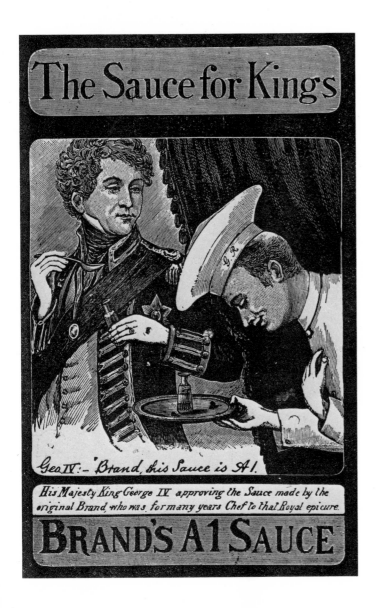

'The Sauce for Kings'. Ad. 1905. Brand & Co., Ltd

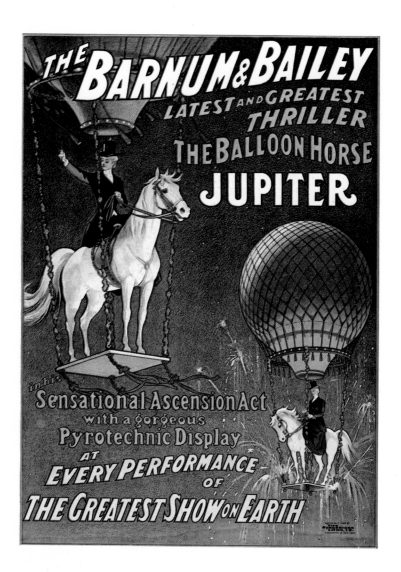

LEFT:
Greatest Show on Earth. Poster. Strobridge artist. 1909.
Barnum & Bailey Circus

ABOVE:
L'Hippodrome, equestrian spectacle. Poster. Manuel Orazi.
c. 1905. L'Hippodrome, Paris

OPPOSITE RIGHT:
U. of P. Poster. J. C. Leyendecker. 1906. University of Pennsylvania

OPPOSITE:
Cycles Gladiator. Poster. Massias. c. 1905.
Cycles Gladiator, Paris

Chérubin, musical comedy. Poster. Maurice Leloir. 1905. Théâtre National de l'Opéra Comique, Paris

Dick Whittington, Christmas pantomime. Poster. c. 1906.
Drury Lane Theatre, London

The Blue Moon, musical play. Postcard.
E. P. Kinsella. 1905. The Lyric Theatre, London

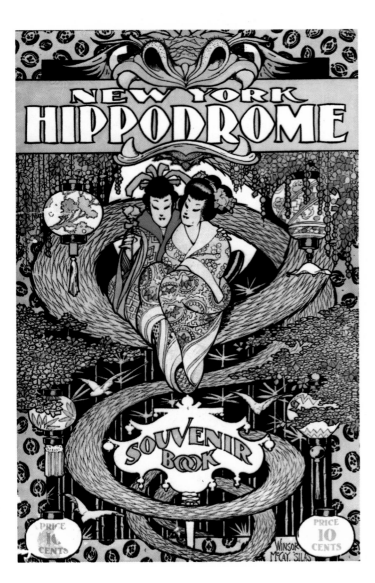

New York Hippodrome Souvenir Book. Cover
(Messrs Lee and J. J. Shubert's 1909–1910 season).
Winsor McCay 'Silas'. c. 1909. Comstock & Gest Inc

Quaker Oats cereal. Ad. 1902. Quaker Oats Company

It Puts Off Old Age

by nourishing the entire system.

Quaker Oats makes your blood tingle; nerves strong and steady; brain clear and active; muscles powerful. It makes flesh rather than fat, but enough fat for reserve force.

It builds children up symmetrically into brainy and robust men and women.

You can work on **Quaker Oats** It stays by you.

At all grocers in 2 lb. Packages only.

Skegness is *So* Bracing. Poster. John Hassall. 1908.
London & North-Eastern Railway

Pettijohn's Breakfast Food. Ad. Paul E. Derrick Advertising.
c. 1905. The American Cereal Co

That satisfied—well-fed feeling.

There's a satisfied—well-fed feeling after a breakfast of delicious Pettijohn's. It satisfies that natural craving for wholesome food. Pettijohn's is a rich full-flaked wheat food, not an illogical granular or powdered wheat that cooks into a tasteless, starchy mass. Pettijohn's is full-flaked. It never deceives.

Besides being an easily and quickly prepared breakfast dish, delicate, appetizing and nourishing, Pettijohn's Breakfast Food makes unequalled **Griddle Cakes, Gems, Muffins** and **Puddings.** Also an excellent thickening for **Soups.** Cold Pettijohn's Porridge is delicious when fried like corn-meal mush. Write for our Cereal Cook Book, edited by Mrs. Rorer. It tells all about cooking all kinds of cereals all sorts of ways. Sent free, postpaid.
THE AMERICAN CEREAL CO.,   Monadnock Bldg., Chicago, Ill.

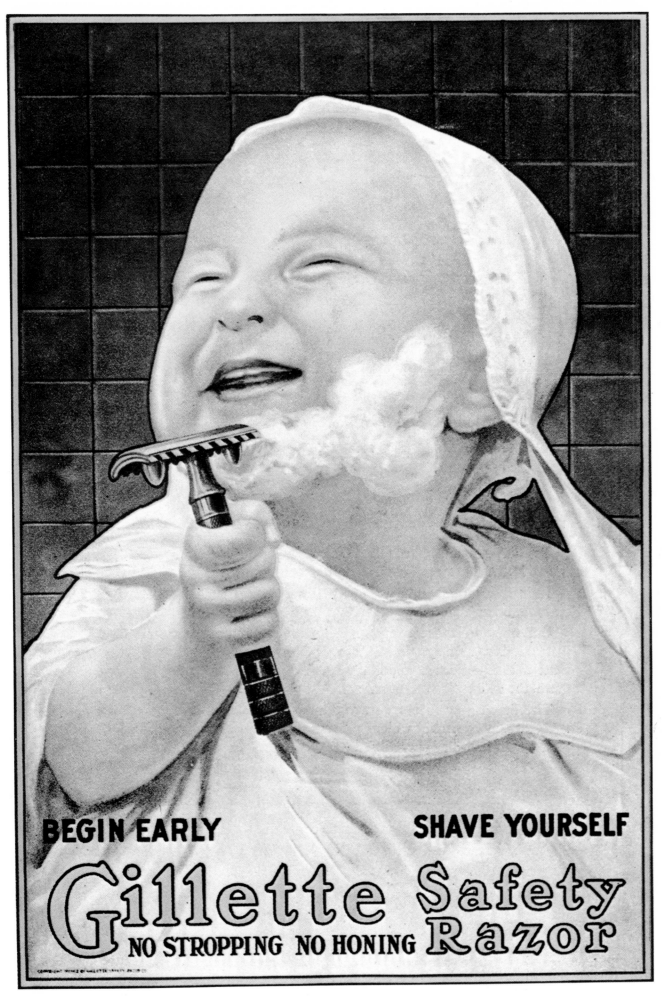

Gillette Safety Razor. Ad. 1905. The Gillette Safety Razor Co

The Sketch magazine. Cover. 1907. The Illustrated London News and Sketch, Ltd

Lux, cleansing solution. Ad. 1902. Lever Brothers Limited

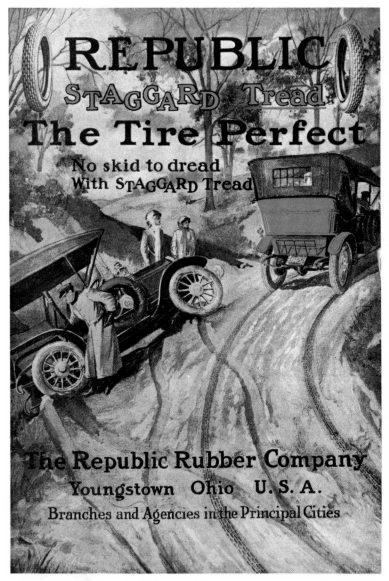

Republic Staggard Tread tires. Ad. c. 1906. The Republic Rubber Company

De Bion Bouton. Poster. H. Thinet. 1903. De Bion Bouton Cars

Century magazine. Cover. Robert J. Wildhack. 1908.
The Century Magazine Co

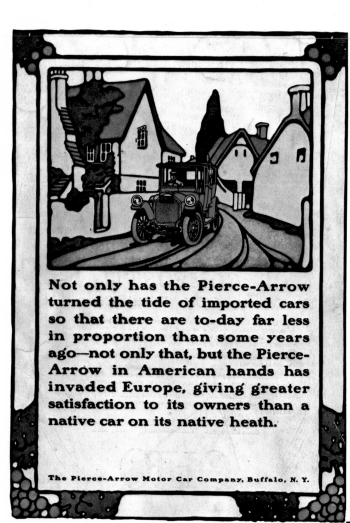

Not only has the Pierce-Arrow turned the tide of imported cars so that there are to-day far less in proportion than some years ago—not only that, but the Pierce-Arrow in American hands has invaded Europe, giving greater satisfaction to its owners than a native car on its native heath.

The Pierce-Arrow Motor Car Company, Buffalo, N. Y.

Pierce-Arrow. Ad. Guernsey Moore. 1913.
The Pierce-Arrow Motor Car Company

Opel. Poster. Hans Rudi Erdt. 1911. Opel Motor Cars

OPPOSITE:
Collier's magazine. Cover ('The Idiot', or 'The Booklover').
Maxfield Parrish. September 24, 1910. P. F. Collier & Son

Along the Coast on Southern Seas. Ad. 1910. Southern Pacific Steamship Lines

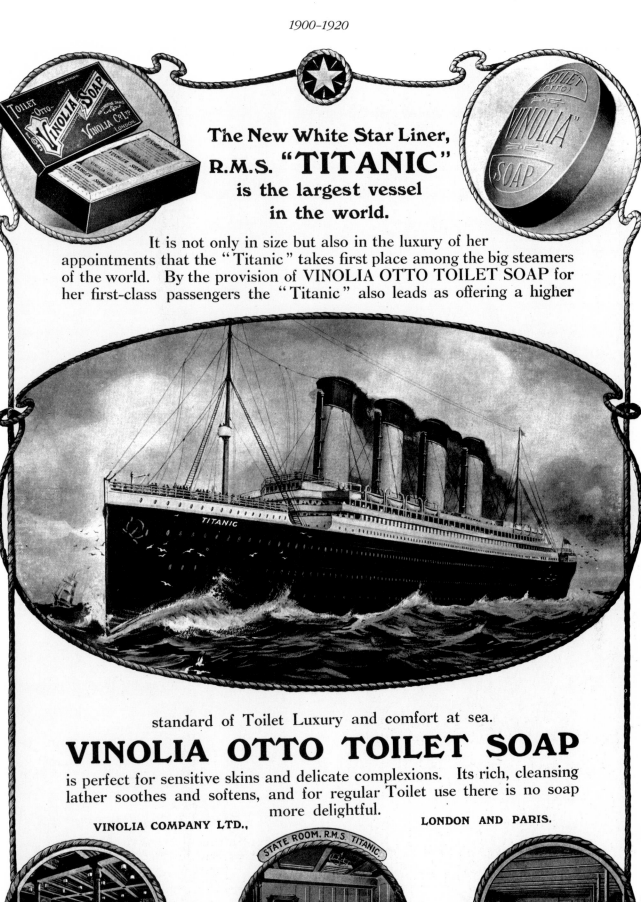

The New White Star Liner,
R.M.S. "TITANIC"
is the largest vessel
in the world.

It is not only in size but also in the luxury of her appointments that the "Titanic" takes first place among the big steamers of the world. By the provision of VINOLIA OTTO TOILET SOAP for her first-class passengers the "Titanic" also leads as offering a higher

standard of Toilet Luxury and comfort at sea.

VINOLIA OTTO TOILET SOAP

is perfect for sensitive skins and delicate complexions. Its rich, cleansing lather soothes and softens, and for regular Toilet use there is no soap more delightful.

VINOLIA COMPANY LTD.,   LONDON AND PARIS.

Vinolia Otto Toilet Soap. Ad. 1912. Vinolia Company Ltd

PARFUM DES JARDINS D'ARMIDE

PARFUMERIE ORIZA

PARFUMERIE ORIZA

Maison L. LEGRAND,
11, Place de la Madeleine, Paris

Parfum des Jardins d'Armide. Ad. c. 1914. Maison L. Legrand

Diaghilev's Russian Ballet. Poster (detail: Nijinsky in *Le Spectre de la Rose*). Jean Cocteau. 1911. Théâtre de Monte Carlo

Diaghilev's Russian Ballet. Poster (detail: Karsavina in *Le Spectre de la Rose*). Jean Cocteau. 1911. Théâtre de Monte Carlo

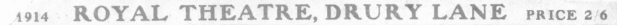

Russian Opera and Ballet: Illustrated Souvenir-Programme. Cover. Léon Bakst/Valentine Gross. 1914. Royal Theatre, London

Heatherbloom petticoats. Ad (Ethel Barrymore).
Ira L. Hill. © 1915. A. G. Hyde & Sons

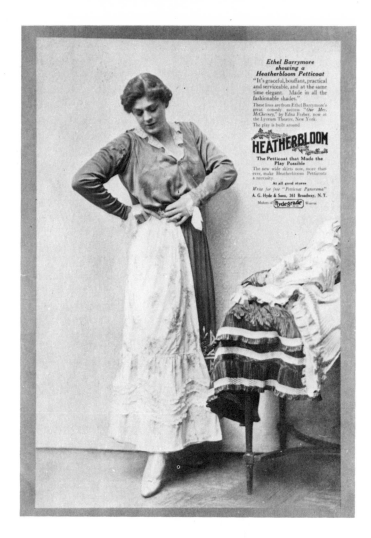

Mrs. Patrick Campbell. Poster. c. 1912.
Liebler & Co., managers

Knox Ladies Hats. Ad (Ina Claire). Ira L. Hill. © 1915. Knox Hats

Mlle. Pavlowa the Incomparable, says:

"It is with pleasure that I state to you that O'Sullivan's Heels of new live rubber give me great comfort in walking. I have them on all my walking shoes and also on a number of my dancing shoes. I recommend them to every member of my company."

O'Sullivan's Heels are made of new *live* rubber —rubber with all the spring in it—and are worn by successful people everywhere.

Ask your bootmaker to attach them, 50c. complete— or you can buy O'Sullivanized Boots and Slippers.

O'Sullivan's Heels. Ad (Anna Pavlova). 1915. O'Sullivan Rubber Corp

Columbia Double-Disc Records. Ad (detail). 1915.
Columbia Gramophone Company

Arrow Collars and Shirts For Dress. Ad.
J. C. Leyendecker. c. 1913. Cluett, Peabody & Co., Inc

'The Gaby Glide' Song sheet, music cover. Starmer. © 1911.
Shapiro Music Publishing Co

THE LADIES' HOME JOURNAL

A ROMANCE AND SOCIAL NUMBER

10 CENTS

THE CURTIS
PUBLISHING COMPANY
PHILADELPHIA

PAINTED BY HARRISON FISHER

FEBRUARY 1, 1911

The Ladies' Home Journal magazine. Cover. Harrison Fisher. 1911. The Curtis Publishing Company

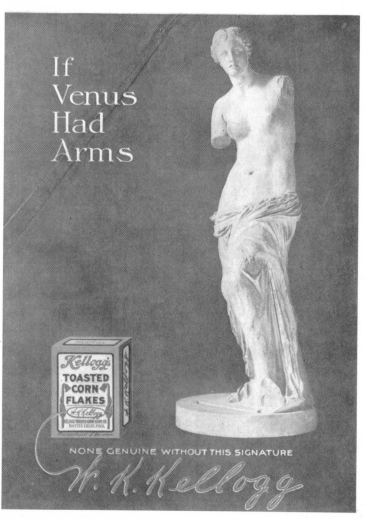

Kellogg's Toasted Corn Flakes. Ad. 1911.
The Kellogg Company

Hermann Scherrer, tailored clothes. Poster.
Ludwig Hohlwein. 1911. Hermann Scherrer

Life magazine, competition. Ad (detail).
Charles Dana Gibson. 1915. Life Publishing Corporation

OPPOSITE:
"Onyx" Silk Hosiery. Ad. 1915. Lord & Taylor, New York

BEFORE YOU LEAVE FOR YOUR VACATION

see that your hosiery wants are supplied in the very newest and most desirable numbers of

 "Onyx" Silk Hosiery

With the "POINTEX" Heel

No matter where you live you will find good selections at your favorite dealers
because leading stores throughout the country feature the "ONYX" brand.

You will find "Onyx," the quality hose, at all quality shops throughout America. If you have difficulty obtaining your exact requirements—let us help you!

Wholesale   **Lord & Taylor**   *New York*

Recruitment poster. c. 1914. Parliamentary Recruiting Committee, London

Home on Leave, play. Poster. 1916. Royalty Theatre, London

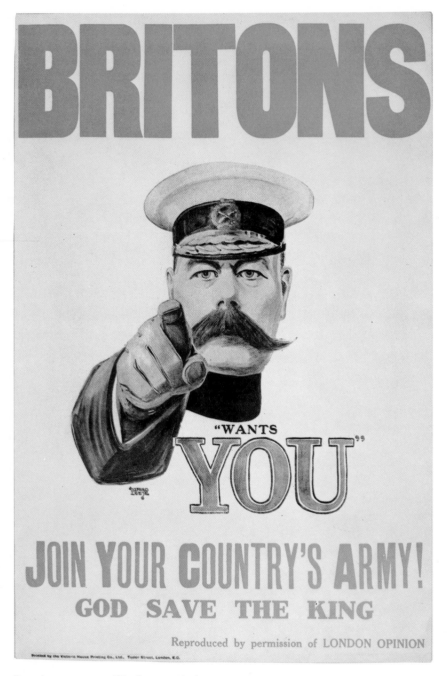

Recruitment poster. Alfred Leete. 1914. Parlimentary Recruiting Committee, London

Recruitment poster. Howard Chandler Christy. 1918.
United States Navy

Recruitment poster. James Montgomery Flagg. 1917.
United States Army

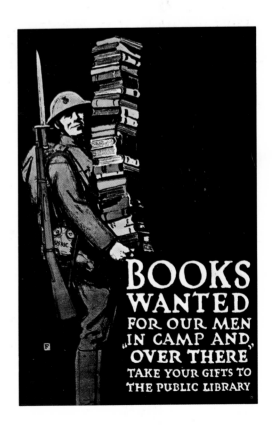

Books Wanted For Our Men. Poster. Charles Buckles Falls.
1918. The American Library Association.

Look for this Trade Mark in your Shoes

F.B.&C.
KID
NEW-YORK
TRADE MARK REGISTERED
UNITED STATES PATENT OFFICE

"Mine are the shoes with 'F. B & C.' in them, porter."

"There must be a lot 'er ladies with names like yours. Mos' all these shoes got 'F. B & C.' in 'em."

"Short skirts for Fall," says Dame Fashion.

Shoes will be in evidence. That means selecting colors in footwear that harmonize.

"F. B & C." is the final word in Quality leather and its remarkable Style appeal lies not only in its beauty of finish, but in the *wide range of colors in which it is shown.*

"'F. B & C.' fits on the Foot like a glove on the hand."

The illustrated pamphlet "Foot Notes" is a revelation of Fashion's secrets in Fall Shoe Styles. We'll send you one on request.

Fashion Publicity Company

Department L   New York City

WASHABLE
"F.B&C."
KID
WHITE GLAZED
Reg U S Pat Off

This Trade Mark shown in   White Washable Kid Shoes

FLATO

© FASHION PUBLICITY COMPANY

'F. B. & C.' Kid shoes. Ad. Flato. © 1919. Fashion Publicity Company

ROLLS-ROYCE

" The Best Car in the World "

Telegrams :
ROLHEAD, LONDON

ROLLS-ROYCE, LIMITED
14 & 15 CONDUIT STREET, LONDON, W

Telephone :
GERRARD 1654 (3 lines)

PARIS ∴ NEW YORK ∴ PETROGRAD AND BOMBAY

Rolls-Royce. Ad. 1917. Rolls-Royce, Limited

$1485 *Milburn* $1485
f. o. b. Toledo *f. o. b. Toledo*
LIGHT ELECTRIC

NEVER was any other Electric such an unqualified success as the 1915 Milburn.

Never before was there such beauty, such style, such comfort, such lightness, such speed and mileage, at anywhere near the price $1485.

This season there are many improvements.

The Milburn is no faster than ever and it now travels even more miles per charge.

And many minor refinements make it a smarter and even more efficient car.

Though Milburn lightness caused a general lightening of Electrics, the Milburn is still by far the lightest.

Though the Milburn price caused a general lowering of prices, the Milburn is still by far the lowest cost Electric—both first cost and operating cost. See the Milburn dealer at once.

Write to us for our catalogue.

THE MILBURN WAGON COMPANY
Established 1848

The Milburn Electric Charger solves the home-charging problem—effectively—inexpensively—if your public garage is inconveniently located or lacking in electric facilities.

TOLEDO, OHIO

Milburn Light Electric. Ad. 1916.
The Milburn Wagon Company

Cheney Silks. Ad. 1918. Cheney Bros., Inc

'Le Lilas de Rigaud' perfume. Marty. Ad (detail).
Rigaud, Paris and London

"Niagara Maid" Underwear. Ad. 1917. Niagara Silk Mills

THE HELPER

Painted by Edward V. Brewer for Cream of Wheat Co.

Copyright 1916 by Cream of Wheat Co.

FREE OFFER

Any Community Silver customer can obtain *free* this Coles Phillips poster, with another in color. These posters contain no reading or advertising matter, and are printed on plate paper in a size suitable for framing.

Ask your silverware dealer to show you these pictures and to get them for you.

COPYRIGHT, 1911
By ONEIDA COMMUNITY, LTD

COLES PHILLIPS

"Are your pink ears listening, Betty?"

"Yes indeed. Will they hear something nice?"

"Better than nice—it's true. Betty, are pearls any less lovely because they all have a grain of sand at the center?"

"No, but what of—?"

"Then how is table silver the worse for having a center of different metal?"

"Well I somehow feel—"

"Pardon me, dear, but that's just it: you only *'feel.'* If you will just stop to *reason* a little you will see that table silver is for a purpose. If it fits that purpose gracefully and completely, I'm for it. Let me read you this:

COMMUNITY SILVER

is built by overlaying solid silver upon a center of stronger, stiffer metal. Do not confuse it with ordinary 'plated' silver, for Community Silver is so specially thickened at the wearing-points, and toughened to withstand wear, that in a long lifetime you will never see or touch anything but the purest of pure silver. *It is guaranteed for 50 years.* There are many attractive designs at your dealer's. The price is attractive, too. For instance, six teaspoons, $2.00."

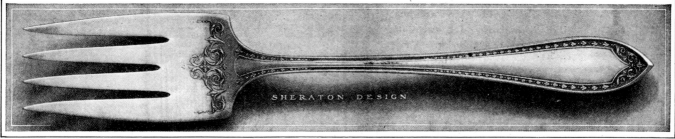

SHERATON DESIGN

ONEIDA COMMUNITY, Ltd.

Community Silver. Ad. Coles Phillips. 1911. Oneida Community, Ltd

Cream of Wheat, breakfast food. Ad. Edward V. Brewer. © 1916. Cream of Wheat Co

A Wonderful example of the value of

OXO

In sight of land

Sole Proprietors and Manufacture

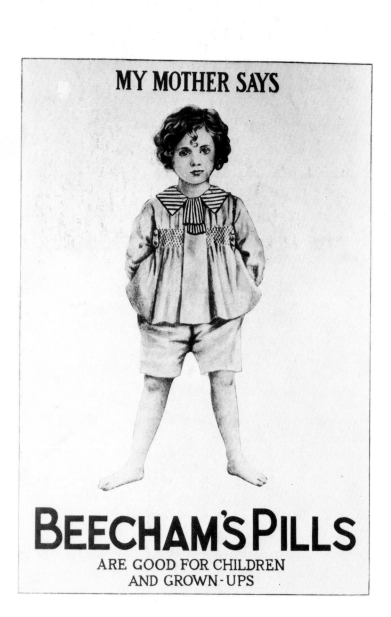

MY MOTHER SAYS

BEECHAM'S PILLS

ARE GOOD FOR CHILDREN
AND GROWN-UPS

LEFT:
Beecham's Pills. Ad. 1919.

ABOVE:
Oxo, beef extract. Ad. 1919. Oxo Limited

OPPOSITE:
Michelin tires (Bibendum). Poster. Gilbert Prilibert.
c. 1918. Michelin Company

OPPOSITE RIGHT:
Drudgery has vanished . . . Ad. 1918. General Electric Company

FIRST NON-STOP FLIGHT ACROSS THE ATLANTIC.

1,960 miles in 15 hours 57 minutes.

Interesting Letter from Captain Sir J. Alcock, K.B.E., D.S.C.

"You will be interested to learn that OXO was a great help to us during our Trans-Atlantic Flight; it sustained us wonderfully during our 16 hours' journey.

"We had found out what a good thing it is when flying in France, and so decided to carry it with us on this occasion, and we can assure you that hot OXO is most acceptable under such cold and arduous conditions. OXO was the only article of its kind which we carried."

J. ALCOCK, Capt., D.S.C.

THAMES HOUSE, LONDON, E.C. 4.

Drudgery has Vanished
Since Electricity came into the home

THE four walls of the kitchen no longer hold the American housewife in solitary confinement. She is younger for her years than ever before. She works less and gets more done. The afternoons and evenings that she always needed and never had, are now hers—for her children, her shopping, her friends. Leisure is hers if she wants it.

The modern servant, Electricity, washes the dishes and clothes, cleans the house thoroughly, grinds meat, turns the ice cream freezer, runs the sewing machine and cools the house in summer. It makes coffee and toast at the dining table, does the cooking "by wire" in a clean, comfortable kitchen, and relieves washing day of its toil.

Electric Heat, Electric Power and Electric Light in the home are responsible for most of the efficiencies and economies that have made the art of housekeeping a modern science.

The development of the MAZDA Lamp from Mr. Edison's invention is an example of what the General Electric Company has done for lighting. Almost as remarkable have been the advances this company has made in perfecting the electric cooking range and applying the electric motor to housework.

You will find a G-E Motor in the best vacuum cleaners, in the best washing machines, and in many other domestic power appliances.

The switches on the wall, sending electricity instantly to its task in response to the touch of your finger; the sockets, plugs, concealed wiring and safety devices; the meter that measures the current—these and many other adjuncts of electric service in the home are products of the General Electric Company, and are so marked.

To the entire electrical industry belongs the credit for putting Electricity to work in the home. But the guiding influence has been that electrical manufacturer whose production services, engineering resources, research, invention and vision have been most useful as the stabilizing and inspirational force of this expanding industry.

GENERAL ELECTRIC COMPANY
· · SCHENECTADY, NEW YORK · ·

MICHELIN

Never Before Such An Instantaneous Success

Never before has an automobile success been so rapid, so definite and so sweeping.

The $615 Overland has made history. It marks the entrance of a new automobile value — a car complete in every sense of the term at a price which was hitherto thought impossible.

Yet here it is — a powerful five passenger touring car *complete* for only $615.

It is large enough for the whole family — moderately priced, within the reach of the majority — economical to maintain — built of the best quality materials — snappy, stylish and speedy — and complete in every sense.

In short, it is just another striking example of how our large production enables us to build a bigger and better car and still keep the price within reason.

You'll want one, so order it now.

Then in a few days you and your whole family will be driving your own car.

Remember it comes complete — only $615!

Catalog on request.   Please address Dept. 617

The Willys-Overland Company, Toledo, Ohio

"Made in U. S. A."

Overland. Ad. Coles Phillips. 1916. The Willys-Overland Company

Luxite Hosiery. Ad. Coles Phillips. 1918. Luxite Textiles, Inc

Luxite Hosiery

UXITE HOSIERY leaves nothing to be desired in either durability or style. This hosiery has an air about it that is charming and refreshing. It seems to say of those who wear it—"This man knows clothes." Or, "Here is a woman of exquisite taste."

These hose improve with acquaintance, not only because they are shapely and resplendent, but because they retain their beauty regardless of how much they are laundered. Luxite Hosiery is alway pure dyed.

Men's and women's styles are made of pure Japanese silk—many strands to the thread. Also of fine lisle, mercerized cotton and Gold-Ray (scientific silk) for men, women and children.

The principal stores can supply you. The few who do not have these hose in stock can get them for you if you insist—and you should. For once you know Luxite you won't be content with ordinary hosiery.

LUXITE TEXTILES, Inc., 636 Fowler Street, Milwaukee, Wisconsin
Makers of High Grade Hosiery Since 1875

NEW YORK   **CHICAGO**   **SAN FRANCISCO**   **LIVERPOOL**

Vim Cleanser and Polisher. Ad. G. Studdy. 1919. Lever Brothers Limited

Jack of Hearts

When he stole those tarts he gave no thought to consequences or to his clothes. He knew he was comfortable, even though he was dressed up, and that's all he cared. Sometimes he's warned to be careful of his clothes, but he has learned that his suits of Indian Head have no such unpleasant restrictions.

For Indian Head launders well; its clean white beauty is fully restored with each tubbing. It gives long service. It tailors well and has an air of smart distinction whether used for sport clothes, children's garments, or table linen.

Indian Head is sold at all good stores in 27, 33, 36, 44, and 54 inch widths. "Indian Head" is always on the selvage. Prices range from 30c to 59c per yard. Booklet with sample on request.

Amory, Browne & Co.

Department 228, Box 1206, Boston, Mass.

*Nashua Blankets   Gilbrae Ginghams   Parkhill Ginghams
Lancaster Kalburnie Ginghams*

INDIAN HEAD CLOTH

Reg. U.S. Pat. Off.

Always on the Selvage

Indian Head Cloth. Ad. M. C. Woodbury. 1919. Amory, Browne & Co

Scranton Filet Nets and Lace Curtains. Ad.
The Reeses. 1918. The Scranton Lace Co

LEFT:
Palace Hotel. Poster. Emile Cardinaux. 1916.
Palace Hotel, St. Moritz

Wells Fargo, travelers' checks. Poster. © 1917.
Wells Fargo & Company

DEL MONTE
CANNED PINEAPPLE

Sun-Ripened, Golden Lusciousness

Nothing more appetizing as a fruit for breakfast—more delicious as a dessert—or as a salad for lunch or dinner.

DEL MONTE Pineapple is Hawaiian, and the very best of Hawaiian. Picked, just when the warm tropical sun has perfectly matured its natural lusciousness, it is immediately packed in pure sugar syrup and its own delicious juice, in such a way that *all* the flavor and fragrance of the sun-ripened fruit is preserved for you.

Insist upon the DEL MONTE Kind at your grocer's. The red DEL MONTE Shield on every can is not only your guarantee of *Hawaii's best pineapple*, but it stands for goodness, purity and quality on a complete line of California canned fruits and vegetables, jams, jellies and preserves, olives, catsup, raisins and many other varieties.

You will find many original and appetizing ways of serving DEL MONTE Canned Pineapple in—

"GOOD THINGS TO EAT"—*A 64-page book in colors of new and unusual recipes. This book, by the well-known cooking expert, Marion Harris Neil, is a revelation of the innumerable ways of preparing tempting and delicious desserts and salads from* DEL MONTE *canned fruits and vegetables. Send 10 cents in stamps addressed to Dept. A.*

CALIFORNIA PACKING CORPORATION
San Francisco, California

Del-Monte Canned Pineapple. Ad. 1918. California Packing Corporation

Harper's Bazar magazine. Cover. Erté. 1918. Hearst Magazines

ARMAND'S COMPLEXION POWDER
In·The·LITTLE·PINK·&·WHITE·BOX

JUST as women had decided that they simply couldn't find a face powder that would "stay on"—along came Armand's in the little Pink and White Box.

Armand's is soft as thistledown, as fragrant as dewdrenched blossoms. It clings to your skin through hours of shopping, outdoor activity and evening gayeties.

Armand's "Tint Natural" blends with all flesh tones, except the deep brunette. Other Armand tints are Brunette, White, Pink and Crème.

The little Pink and White Hat Box filled with Armand's "Aida," the "cold creamy" out-door powder—sells for $1.00. The oval box, with "Amabelle" fragrance, sells at 75c, and the square box perfumed with "Bouquet" at 50c. The Powder itself is the same at all prices— it has the same soft clinging qualities. Indicate your choice and a guest room box of Armand's Powder will be mailed upon receipt of 10c in stamps.

THE ARMAND COMPANY,   DES MOINES, IOWA.

Since May 29, 1916, the genuineness of each and every package of Armand's Powder is assured by the following trade-marks—Louis XVI Silhouette Medallion; Armand Signature; and red and white check blue stripe design.

Armand's Complexion Powder. Ad. Edward A. Wilson. 1918. The Armand Company

Old Dutch Cleanser

Chases Dirt

MAKES EVERYTHING "SPICK AND SPAN"

Cleanliness
brings
Happiness
and
Good Cheer

A Merry Christmas
and
A Happy New Year

yours
"Old Dutch"

1919
"On your way home from School, be sure to call at the Grocer's in New Street for my Sunlight Soap."

£1000 SUNLIGHT SOAP · GUARANTEE OF PURITY

1969 *"On your way home from the Academy of Futurist Philosophy, be sure to call at the Store in 41st Street for my Sunlight Soap."*

Education endorses the worth of SUNLIGHT SOAP

Time cannot improve upon it.

LEVER BROTHERS LIMITED, PORT SUNLIGHT.

Sunlight Soap. Ad. 1919. Lever Brothers Limited

Old Dutch Cleanser. Ad. 1919. Purex Corporation Ltd

1920-1940

The Great War was followed by two years of feverish prosperity, then suddenly business slumped, unemployment rose, and strikes broke out.

Lloyd George, who with Woodrow Wilson and Georges Clemenceau witnessed the signing of the Peace Treaty at Versailles on June 28, 1919, remained England's Prime Minister in 1920. But Wilson, whose dedication to the League of Nations had not been supported by the U. S. Senate, suffered a stroke in September 1919, living on to see Warren Harding—whose 'bungalow mind' he deplored—elected President of an isolationist United States.

Business was in trouble. The war had upset the world's economy, and the defeated nations were without money. England alone had lost a million men, and the young, sickened by the results of a 'senseless war', closed their eyes to the past and were determined to have a good time.

'I Want to Be Happy' and 'Do Do Do' were in tune with the times. Jazz—straight, Gershwin, or Paul Whiteman's symphonic jazz—was all the young wanted to listen to, and with Gramophones, Victrolas, and now the radio as well, they so easily could.

A popular spokesman for the new age was F. Scott Fitzgerald, who entered wholeheartedly into what he described as 'America's greatest and giddiest spree in history'. In 1925 his third novel, *The Great Gatsby,* was a best-seller; so, that year, were Aldous Huxley's *Those Barren Leaves,* Anita Loos' *Gentlemen Prefer Blondes,* and Sinclair Lewis's *Arrowsmith.*

In celebration of the emancipation of women Paris tossed the corset to the winds and introduced the boyish, clothespin silhouette, with short skirts, bobbed hair, plucked eyebrows, and lips crimsoned to a cupid's bow. What a witty cleric called 'a pandemonium of powder, a riot of rouge, and moral anarchy of dress' was, when accompanied by the magnetism of a Clara Bow, what novelist Elinor Glyn called It. Long earrings were the height of fashion (page 83); so were long cigarette holders and even longer necklaces (page 112).

Fancy dress balls had their enthusiasts, but instead of Venus, Cleopatra, or Marie Antoinette being circled round and round to a waltz by Strauss, the ladies of history were now happily backed around the room to a fox-trot, turned smartly sideways to dip into a tango, or let loose to take, as an evangelical follower of Aimee Semple McPherson said, 'the first and easiest step to hell', doing the Charleston (page 112) or Black Bottom.

Prohibition, which became law in 1920, produced exactly opposite results to those intended. Speakeasies multiplied, enjoyed by the new 'cocktail' crowd who responded to the dare of illegal drinking, even at the risk of drinking the bootleg brew that poisoned some two thousand Americans in 1926.

The golden-haired boys of business were the salesman and the ad man. With more styles of everything from cars to cosmetics, super salesmanship and clever advertising were the only ways to beat the competition. For example, the personal endorsement of a soap or cosmetic by a famous beauty, implying that you too could look as terrific as, say, Lady Diana Manners (page 115), was a new and highly successful sales pitch.

Instalment buying, started in a small way in 1915, was now widespread. To some, 'Enjoy now, pay later' sounded like a pact with the devil, but to the masses signing a slip of paper and driving off in a brand-new car was heaven.

The growing success of motion pictures profited other industries besides Hollywood. Millions were spent building chains of 'movie palaces', and more millions advertising 'coming attractions'—Douglas Fairbanks in *The Thief of Bagdad* (page 86), for example, or Charlie Chaplin in *The Kid* (page 86), or a new film with the great Garbo, the most glamorous of all 'silent' stars to triumph equally in sound (page 119).

The first talkie, *The Jazz Singer,* was filmed in 1927, a good year for both jazz and musical comedy. *A Connecticut Yankee* and *Good News!* (page 112) were big successes. So were Fred and Adele Astaire in *Funny Face,* tap-dancing to Gershwin's 'S'wonderful'—with Fray and Braggiotti at the orchestra's two grand pianos—a sensation no one who experienced it could ever forget. In 1930 the Astaires were at it again in *The Band Wagon* (page 121).

The year 1927 also became a historic one in the air as Charles Lindbergh made the first solo transatlantic flight. Then in 1928 the Germans sent the Graf Zeppelin across the Atlantic, heralding a passenger air service (page 147) that was to last until the *Hindenburg* exploded over New Jersey in 1937. While local airplane passenger service was common, transatlantic travel still

meant booking on the new *Queen Mary,* the *Normandie* (page 136), or another great liner and getting a rousing send-off with streamers and jazz band.

The prosperity of the late twenties, in America particularly, where even elevator boys bought stocks on margin, hoping to become Rockefellers overnight, ended with the Wall Street Crash of 1929. The ensuing Great Depression in America, and the less violent slump in England, where James Ramsay MacDonald headed a coalition government, brought unemployment problems and breadlines. Paris, as if in mourning for the good old flapper days, lowered ladies' skirts to half-mast.

In 1932 the election of Franklin D. Roosevelt and his 'New Deal' platform led to Social Security, the repeal of Prohibition, and a gradual return to prosperity as vast projects like the Works Progress Administration (W.P.A.) got under way.

In advertising, the high standard set by Frank Pick and his London Underground artists inspired England's big railways to engage fine artists like Frank Taylor. The work of Tom Purvis, Austin Cooper, Francis Marshall, and Ashley Havinden was to be seen everywhere. Two of the most successful campaigns ever brought fun to the sombre thirties: 'That's Shell—That Was' (page 145) by poster artist John Gilroy, and 'My Goodness, My Guinness' by John Reynolds (page 138). In America the realistic style of Willy Pogany, Norman Rockwell, T. M. Cleland, and J. C. Leyendecker remained popular, while Vienna's Joseph Binder introduced to America an exciting new concept of poster design. In Europe A. M. Cassandre became as great an influence on the art of the poster as McKnight Kauffer. Important photographers entering the increasingly competitive advertising field included Edward Steichen, Herbert Matter, and Martin Munkacsi. All the above are represented in the following illustrations.

On the darker side, the early thirties saw the growing strength of Hitler and Mussolini, and Spain's civil war. The turbulent times found more people reading novels and going to the movies. The best-selling novel of the thirties was Margaret Mitchell's *Gone With the Wind,* which in 1939 became one of the most successful films ever, with Clark Gable as Rhett and Vivien Leigh as Scarlett, although the New York critics gave an even higher 'year's best' rating to *Wuthering Heights,* with Laurence Olivier and Merle Oberon.

On stage in London Charles B. Cochran was producing sophisticated revues at the Pavilion in Piccadilly Circus. John Gielgud became the greatest Hamlet, the Lunts the most popular husband-and-wife stage team. In 1934 Cole Porter wrote *Anything Goes.* Noel Coward was in his heyday: after *Bitter Sweet* came his *Private Lives* with Gertrude Lawrence as Amanda (page 127). J. B. Priestley was writing a new play almost every year. Rudolf Besier's *The Barretts of Wimpole Street* starred Gwen Ffrangcon-Davies in London and Katharine Cornell in New York. Eugene O'Neill followed *Mourning Becomes Electra* with *Ah! Wilderness,* and Maxwell Anderson's play *Mary of Scotland* saw Helen Hayes as Mary onstage and Katharine Hepburn in the same role in the 1936 film.

Threats of war continued to multiply, but even Hitler (page 148) took second place in the headlines as England's royal drama began to unfold. After George V died, in January 1936, Edward VIII became King, but before the year was out he had abdicated to marry the twice-divorced Wallis Simpson of Baltimore.

Edward's brother, George VI, was crowned in 1937, and two years later, he and his Queen Elizabeth became the first reigning English monarchs to see the U.S.A.—enjoying hot dogs with the Roosevelts and visiting the New York World's Fair (page 146). Later that year England was again at war with Germany.

FROM LEFT TO RIGHT:

John Barrymore in *Hamlet.* Detail from a poster by E. Cadmus. 1922
Poster for the motion picture *Son of the Sheik.* 1926
Edward McKnight Kauffer's new cover for *The Studio.* 1929
Franklin D. Roosevelt. Photographed by Edward Steichen in 1929
King Edward VIII with the Duke of York and the Duke of Gloucester at the funeral of their father, George V. 1936
Poster for David O. Selznick's *Gone With the Wind.* 1939

Will a Corset Stand It?

YOU expect much of a corset! You lace it hurriedly in the morning and keep it on till night. You lean over the oven—it must bend. You frolic with the baby—it must yield with every movement. You take violent exercise—it must withstand every lurch and twist!

Will a corset that is made to give style and comfort hold up under all this?

A Warner's Rust-Proof Corset will. It has been made to withstand every strain. The boning is double, which means that it will bend to every movement but will not remain bent. It holds the shape of the corset but adds nothing to the weight.

Your Warner's Rust-Proof need never be discolored or soiled. For you can wash it as often as you like.

Every Warner's Rust-Proof Corset is guaranteed not to rust, break or tear.★

Under the comfortable firmness of a Warner's Rust-Proof, hips disappear. It is the underlying secret of many a trim tailored suit and soft, clinging gown!

Comfort, style, double wear, double life, real economy—all this you find in a Warner's Rust-Proof Corset.

★
REMEMBER!
Warner's Rust-Proof is the guaranteed corset

Warner's
Rust-Proof
Corsets—

Warner's Rust-Proof Corsets. Ad. 1920. The Warner Bros. Co

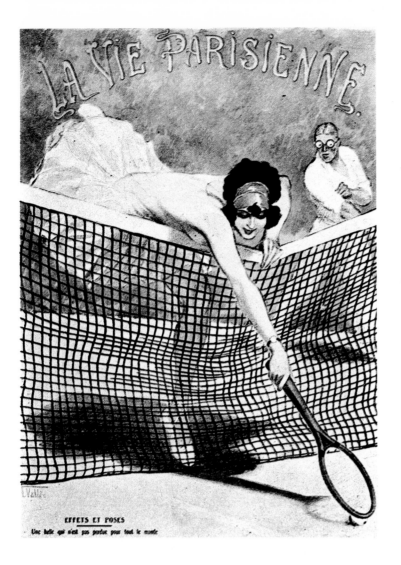

La Vie Parisienne magazine. Cover. L. Vallée. c. 1921.
La Vie Parisienne

Gainsborough Genuine Hair Net. Ad. Andrew Loomis. 1922.
The Western Company

Holeproof Hosiery. Ad. Coles Phillips. © 1921.
Holeproof Hosiery Company

FOR EACH NEW STYLE *a Silk by Corticelli*

These photographs by Campbell Studios   *Posed by Irene Castle*

Lucile uses Corticelli Satin Crêpe to create this gorgeous evening gown for Irene Castle. Rhinestone ornaments serve to accent its richness. The sleeve and train give a bizarre note that lends to the gown added distinction.

This afternoon frock of the new Corticelli Castle Duvene in the Wallflower shade expresses the possibilities of this delightful new silk. This costume is also most effective in the new Muffin shade which Paris is featuring. Corticelli Crêpe de Chine, hand-embroidered, is used for the collar and cuffs.

T HIS season Paris devotes herself to fabrics—no less so America. True to their tradition, the makers of Corticelli Dress Silks give you a great profusion of new silks. Whether you demand simplicity or extreme novelty—whether you are planning a street frock or an elaborate evening gown, you will find among the Corticelli Dress Silks one which is most appropriate. If your favorite store cannot show you Corticelli Satin Crêpe, Satin Princess, Crêpe de Chine, Taffetas, Castle Duvene, and Castle Co-ket, write us. On request we will gladly advise you where the attractive costumes illustrated on this page may be bought. The Corticelli Silk Company, 109 Nonotuck St., Florence, Mass.

New frocks for Irene Castle

Ask your dealer, or send to us today, for free booklet in full colors showing Irene Castle in fashionable new frocks of Corticelli Dress Silks. It will give you many valuable ideas.

Knitting ideas—wholly new

Corticelli Knitting and Crochet Book No. 19 shows photographs of many exclusive ideas for blouses, tuxedos, dresses, etc., both for grown-ups and youngsters. At your dealer's or by mail, 15 cents.

Irene Castle's tight-fitting blouse and matching coat-lining are of Corticelli Castle Co-ket. The skirt and coat are fashioned of Corticelli Castle Duvene, with trimmings of the fabric itself. Designed by Joseph A. Morris & Co., New York.

THE CORTICELLI SILK COMPANY

Also makers of Corticelli Spool Silks, Ladies' Silk Hosiery, Yarns and Crochet Cottons

Corticelli silk. Ad (Irene Castle). Campbell Studios. 1922. The Corticelli Silk Company

Theatre magazine. Cover. A. J. Knorr. 1923. The Theatre Magazine Company

THEATRE
MAGAZINE

NOVEMBER
1923

35
cents

A·J·Knorr

Why It Costs So Much To Amuse You

REAL Peppermint Flavor

Get the new Wrigley's Double Mint and have a delicious, lasting treat— REAL Peppermint—full strength.

Easy to remember: Double Mint. And hard to forget— once you've tried it.

The *satisfying* confection.

···*After every meal*···

Wrigley's Double Mint Chewing Gum. Ad. 1927. J. M. Wrigley Jr. Company

'F. B. & C.' Kid shoes. Ad (detail). © 1920. Amalgamated Leather Companies, Inc

Kalburnie Gingham. Ad. Edith F. Butler. © 1922. Amory, Browne & Co

Campbell's Condensed Vegetable Soup. Ad (detail). Grace Gebbie Drayton. 1920. Joseph Campbell Company

THE PERFECT PAIR.

Eve and the Tatler

Eve and the *Tatler* magazines. Ad. Mabel Lucie Attwell. 1923. Illustrated Newspapers Ltd

"*Mum*" is the Guardian
of your Personal Daintiness

'Mum', deodorant cream. Ad (detail). 1922.
Mum Manufacturing Co

Douglas Fairbanks in *The Thief of Bagdad*, motion picture.
Poster. Anton Grut. 1924. United Artists Corp

This is the great
picture upon which
the famous comedian
has worked a whole
year.

6 reels of Joy.

Charles Chaplin in *The Kid*, motion picture. Poster. 1920.
First National Motion Pictures Distributors Inc

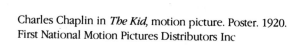

Victrola (Caruso, Melba, Galli-Curci, Farrar, Schumann-Heink, Scotti, and others). Ad. Norman Price. 1922. Victor Talking Machine Company

Life magazine. Cover (detail). F. X. Leyendecker.
© 1922. Life Publishing Co

Abdulla cigarettes. Ad (detail). Lewis Baumer. c. 1923.
Abdulla & Company, Ltd

Springtime is Rug Time. Ad. Willy Pogany. 1929.
Mohawk Carpet Mills

Springtime is Rug Time

It's Spring again! And Mother Nature, wise housekeeper of the great outdoors, makes over her wide domain for another twelvemonth.

You, too, like all good housekeepers, choose Spring as the ideal time to transform that little world of your creation—your home. You realize, of course, that in your scheme of decoration floors are basic, and that nothing can so cheer and freshen your home after weary months of Winter as the laying of a new rug. Indeed, at

this season, a new rug—soft, warm, colorful—seems like a captured fragment of the mantle of Spring itself.

Yes, Springtime is rug time almost everywhere. Surely, it's going to be in *your* home, too! There's a Mohawk dealer near you, ready with the latest Mohawk patterns and colorings in every popular weave to suit your individual taste and needs. And remember: No matter what you wish to pay, your rug can always be a Mohawk.

This Pattern is Akbar Seamless Wilton No. 364A

8 Lessons in Home Decoration

MOHAWK CARPET MILLS
16 Lyon Street
Amsterdam, New York
Gentlemen:
I should like to have...
the revised Mohawk Course in Home... written and...
...in full color by...
...Heisler Button. I...
...10 cents in stamps to cover mailing charges.

Name....................
Street....................
City.............. State..............

MOHAWK RUGS & CARPETS

© 1920. A. H. S. Co.

À une sorcerie féerique seulement pouvez-vous attribuer le charme de mon talc Djer-Kiss — captivant dans son exquisité, captivant dans son charme français — Kerkoff, Paris.

Translation — To faerie magic alone can you impute the charm of my Djer-Kiss Talc — captivating in its exquisiteness, captivating in its French grace.

Djer-Kiss Talc
—the warm summer through

Made in Paris, Djer-Kiss Talc brings to you quite *l'air exquis*, a fascination so quite Parisian. And what a softness and purity — what a fragrance of refinement! With what smoothness *après le bain!* With what a soothingness in warm weather!

Surely, Mademoiselle, more than ever you will love this unusual French Talc — Djer-Kiss Talc — the warm summer through.

Djer-Kiss
Made in France*

EXTRACT ▾ FACE POWDER ▾ TALC ▾ SACHET
TOILET WATER ▾ VEGETALE ▾ SOAP

*ROUGE *LIP STICK *COLD CREAM
Made in America with Djer-Kiss Concentré

In return for fifteen cents the Alfred H. Smith Company, 40 West 34th St., New York City, will be happy to send you samples of Djer-Kiss Extract, **Face Powder** and **Sachet**.

Djer-Kiss talc. Ad. C. F. Neagle. © 1920. The Alfred H. Smith Company

Join the Big Parade. Ad. 1928. Beech-Nut Company

Adams California Fruit Gum. Ad. Neysa McMein. © 1920. American Chicle Co

Had Your Iron Today?

Serve
Energy at Breakfast
for the Benefit of Men

*Athletes know the
energy in Raisins*

Sun-Maid Raisins. Ad (detail). C. E. Ruttan. 1922.
Sun-Maid Raisin Growers

Normal healthy appetites satisfied by
good things to eat from your baker
Fresh every day
GOLD MEDAL FLOUR
used by the best bakers everywhere

WASHBURN'S
Eventually
GOLD MEDAL FLOUR
Why Not Now?

Gold Medal Flour. Ad. René Clarke. 1924.
Washburn-Crosby Co

Fudge—

made with Beech-Nut Peanut Butter! Just the thing
for summer evenings and to have in the house to nibble
on when you yearn for something particularly good.
And the best of it is, this dainty confection is quite easy
to make. Beech-Nut Peanut Butter gives the fudge
a smooth, creamy texture—keeps it free from the
common tendency to become grainy and to crumble.
Moreover, the same tempting flavor that makes
Beech-Nut Peanut Butter such a delicious spread for
bread is simply irresistible in the candy.

Use the recipe given below. It is easy to follow and
yields delicious results.

2 cups brown sugar, ¾ cup
milk, 1 teaspoonful vanilla,
¼ cup Beech-Nut Peanut
Butter. Boil sugar and milk
until it forms a soft ball when

tested in cold water. Cool,
add Peanut Butter and va-
nilla. Beat until creamy—
turn into buttered pan; mark
in squares.

BEECH-NUT
*"Foods and Confections
of Finest Flavor"*

Bacon
Peanut Butter
Macaroni
Spaghetti
Vermicelli
Macaroni Elbows
Macaroni Rings
Prepared Spaghetti
Pork and Beans
Tomato Catsup
Chili Sauce
Prepared Mustard
Jams and Jellies
Marmalades and
    Preserves

CONFECTIONS
Mints
Fruit Drops
Caramels
Chewing Gum

BEVERAGES
Ginger Ale
Birch Beer
Sarsaparilla

**Beech-Nut
Peanut Butter**

BEECH-NUT PACKING COMPANY
CANAJOHARIE, NEW YORK

Beech-Nut Peanut Butter. Ad. Cushman Parker. © 1922.
Beech-Nut Packing Company

For midsummer dinners—Premium Ham!

On hot sultry days how glad you will be to have baked Premium Ham in the ice-box! For a dinner as cooling and welcome as the breeze that ripples through the leaves at the end of the day—serve thin slices of the ham with a crisp salad and an iced drink.

Swift's Premium Ham is the meat of tender plump porkers—skillfully cured and hung over the fragrant smoke of hard wood fires. That is why it has such a refreshing rich delicacy of flavor, such tenderness that it comes apart just at the touch of a fork.

Place a Premium Ham in cold water, heat slowly and simmer gently, allowing about 30 minutes to the pound. Remove the rind; pierce the fat with cloves and bake one hour in a moderate oven.

Swift's Premium Hams and Bacon

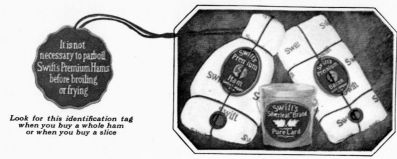

It is not necessary to parboil Swift's Premium Hams before broiling or frying

Look for this identification tag when you buy a whole ham or when you buy a slice

Swift & Company
U. S. A.

Swift's Premium Hams and Bacon. Ad. John Newton Howitt. 1922. Swift & Company

Ransomes, grass machinery. Display card. James Haworth. 1928. Ransomes, Sims and Jefferies Ltd

Dining room in the home of Mr. John M. Hatton, architect, at Scotch Plains, N. J. Notice how the floor of GOLD SEAL INLAID, *Belflor Pattern No. 2047/8, gives unity to the colorful decorative scheme*

Beautiful floors helped restore this architect's home

The same pattern of GOLD SEAL IN-LAIDS *lends a cheerful yet dignified note to the hall furnishings of Mr. Hatton's remodeled home*

Would you ever suspect that the colorful period room shown above is in a remodeled house? To the architect-owner, the floors presented one of the biggest problems in the rejuvenation of the old house. But Nairn GOLD SEAL INLAIDS solved the difficulty—artistically and economically.

In the dining room and hall, a *Belflor* design with softly-mottled gray squares alternating with black squares was used. As you can see in the picture, the floor accents the "Old World" note of the entire setting.

Of course, GOLD SEAL INLAIDS are just as effective in new houses—cottages, apartments or costly residences. Nor are the humbler portions of the house forgotten by Nairn designers. There are GOLD SEAL INLAIDS in solid colored, sharply-defined patterns to add a cheerful touch of neatness to kitchen, bathroom and pantry.

In every GOLD SEAL INLAID the colors go through to the sturdy back. These inlaid linoleum floors are easy to clean; an occasional waxing is all that's needed to keep them in perfect condition.

Although low in price, your complete satisfaction, or your money back, is absolutely guaranteed by the Gold Seal. Look for it on the face of the goods—or the name Nairn on the back.

Free—"Creating a Charming Home"

This new booklet by Laura Hale Shipman contains many interiors in colors and scores of practical suggestions that will help you plan distinctive, colorful rooms for your home. May we send you a free copy?

CONGOLEUM-NAIRN INC.

Philadelphia   New York   Boston   Chicago   Kansas City   Atlanta
Minneapolis   Cleveland   Dallas   Pittsburgh   San Francisco   New Orleans

NAIRN
Gold Seal
INLAID
SATISFACTION GUARANTEED
OR YOUR MONEY BACK
REMOVE SEAL WITH
WET CLOTH

When buying INLAID LINOLEUM ask for NAIRN
GOLD SEAL INLAIDS

Nairn Gold Seal Inlaids. Ad. Meyer. 1926. Congoleum-Nairn Inc

Cashmere Bouquet soap. Ad (detail). Arthur Rackham. 1924.
Colgate & Co

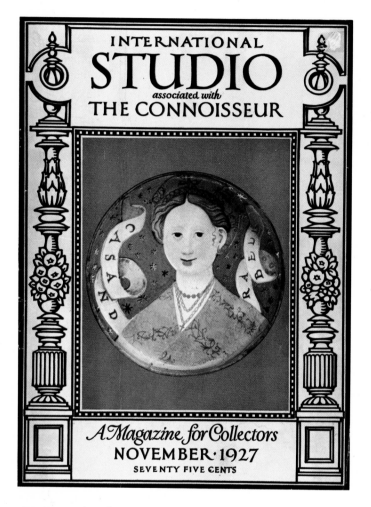

International Studio magazine. Cover. 1927.
Hearst Magazines

Arnold Constable, department store. Ad. Jean Dupas. 1928..
Arnold Constable, New York

Peter Robinson, department store. Catalogue cover. Garth Jones. c. 1924. Peter Robinson Ltd, London

Colgate's Perfumes. Ad. George Sheringham. 1924.
Colgate & Co

Concert Mayol, revue. Programme cover. Barjansky. c. 1928.
O. Dufrenne, Director

Cadbury Sheridan Chocolates. Box label. Freda Beard. 1924.
Cadbury Brothers Ltd

McCallum Silk Hosiery. Ad. Mary MacKinnon. 1922. McCallum Hosiery Company

for Economical Transportation

CHEVROLET

The Most **Beautiful**

CHEVROLET

in Chevrolet History

Brilliant in their modish new colors—alluring in their distinguished smartness, the new Chevrolet models disclose that individuality and perfection of silhouette you would expect to find only in the costliest of custom-built creations.

One of the most revolutionary advancements ever made in the development of the low-priced motor car, the Most Beautiful Chevrolet introduces marvelous new bodies by Fisher with their beauty emphasized by bullet-type lamps and one-piece full-crown fenders. In addition, longer life and better operation are assured by a host of

mechanical improvements, including an oil filter and an air cleaner.

Thus, for the first time there are available at such low prices both that extraordinary ease of handling and that elusive something which women of discrimination have always demanded in a motor car.

Plan to visit the nearest Chevrolet dealer. There a single inspection will reveal how successfully the world's largest builder of gearshift automobiles is maintaining leadership with new models of delightful beauty and amazing value!

CHEVROLET MOTOR COMPANY, DETROIT, MICHIGAN
Division of General Motors Corporation

The Coach

QUALITY AT LOW COST

The Most Beautiful Chevrolet. Ad. 1927. Chevrolet Motor Company

Mavis, talcum and eau de toilette. Ad. Fred L. Packer. 1920. Vivaudou Parfumeurs Inc

PARIS VIVAUDOU NEW YORK
MAVIS
Irresistible!
The delicate freshness of Mavis is like the breath of an April day— for both are fragrant heralds of the flowers of Spring

Lincoln. Ad. 1928. Lincoln Motor Company

Cadillac. Ad. T. M. Cleland. 1928. General Motors Inc

Time to Retire? Ad. Norman Rockwell. 1924.
The Fisk Tire Co., Inc

Take a Kodak With You. Poster (detail). Fred Pegram. 1925. Eastman Kodak Company

Bisto, extract for gravy. Poster. Will Owen. 1929.
Cerebos Limited

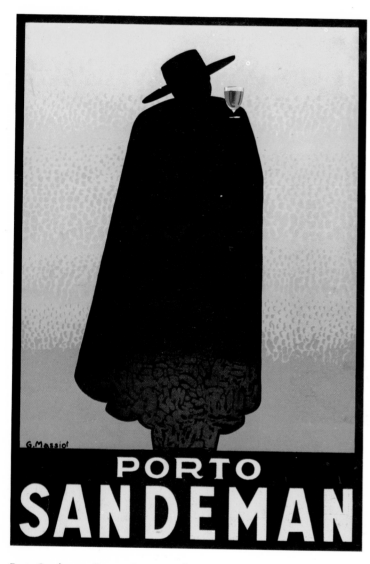

Porto Sandeman. Poster. G. Massiot (George Massiot Brown).
1929. George G. Sandeman & Sons, Co., Ltd

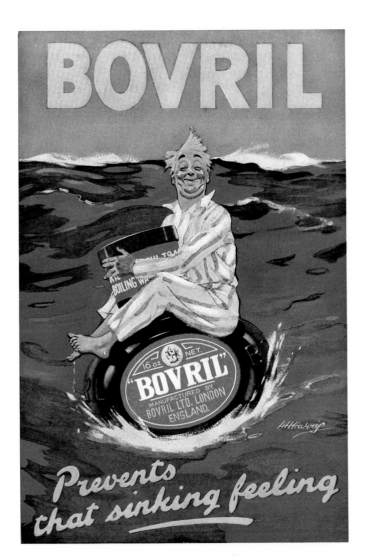

Bovril, beef extract. Poster. H. H. Harris. 1923.
Bovril Ltd

"I must have left it behind!"

Andrews Liver Salt. Ad. John Hassall. 1929.
Scott & Turner Ltd

Prince George Hotel. Poster. F. G. Cooper. 1924.
Prince George Hotel, New York

Mr Pickwick Passing the Ancient House, Ipswich. Poster (detail).
Fred Taylor. c. 1926. London & North-Eastern Railway Company

"My Lady" Fruits. Display card. Edgar Wright. c. 1925.
Angus Watson & Co., Limited

Royal Baking Powder. Ad. Leonetto Capiello. 1923.
Royal Baking Powder Co

OPPOSITE:
Dewar's Whiskey. Ad. W. Dendy Sadler. c. 1926.
John Dewar & Sons Ltd

Copyright 1926 John Dewar & Sons Ltd. U.S.A.

Painted by W. Dendy Sadler. London, Published 1st June 1926 by John Dewar & Sons Ltd. Dewar House, S.W.1. the Proprietors of the Copyright. Etched by C.O. Murray.

"LADIES AND GENTLEMEN."

The Peep-Show, revue. Programme cover. H. Willoughby. 1921.
London Hippodrome

La Plage de Monte Carlo. Poster. Michel Bouchaud. 1929.
Monte Carlo Publicité Vox

Mazda lamps: 'Venetian Lamplighter' Calendar. Maxfield Parrish. 1922.
Edison Lamp Works

108

Vichy festival. Poster. Roger Broders. c. 1926. Vichy Comité des Fêtes

Blondes ~ Brunettes ~ Red-heads

such widely varying types . . .

yet all screen stars alike have the vital appeal of smooth skin

9 *out of* 10 *screen stars keep their skin lovely with Lux Toilet Soap . . .*

AN exquisite velvety skin is any girl's greatest charm, and for the screen star it is *all* important, 39 leading motion picture directors say.

"I don't know a single girl without lovely skin who has won enough of the public to become a star," says William Beaudine, director for Fox.

"Exquisite smooth skin is the all important asset of the star who must face into the glaring lights of the close-up," Joan Crawford explains.

The next time you see any of these lovely screen stars in a close-up, notice how smooth Lux Toilet Soap keeps her skin. "It gives my skin that beautiful smoothness I thought only the finest French soaps gave," Renée Adorée says.

Nine out of ten screen stars are devoted to Lux Toilet Soap, and all the great film studios have made it the official soap for their dressing rooms.

You, too, will like the way this white, daintily fragrant soap lathers so generously even in hard water! It is made by the famous French method. Buy several cakes—today.

BLONDES

Marion Davies says: "I am delighted with Lux Toilet Soap for deliciously smooth 'studio skin.'"

Esther Ralston, Paramount—"It is excellent for keeping the skin delightfully smooth."

Dorothy Mackaill, First National — "Lux Toilet Soap is lovely for the skin."

Anna Q. Nilsson, R.K.O. —"It is a splendid aid in keeping the skin velvety."

BRUNETTES

Bebe Daniels, Paramount —"Lux Toilet Soap helps so much to keep the skin smooth and lovely."

Billie Dove, First National —"I find Lux Toilet Soap delightfully pure and so very refreshing."

Lupe Velez, United Artists, says: "Lux Toilet Soap certainly keeps my skin velvety."

Louise Brooks says: "It gives the skin the satin smoothness a screen star's skin must have."

More of the many stars who use this soap:

BLONDES
Phyllis Haver—Pathé
May McAvoy—Warner Brothers
Jeanette Loff—Pathé
Gilda Gray—Independent
Lois Moran—Fox
Mae Murray—Independent
Greta Nissen—Independent
Vera Reynolds—Independent

BRUNETTES
Madge Bellamy—Fox
Olive Borden—Independent
Mary Duncan—Fox
Marie Prevost—Independent
Aileen Pringle—Metro-Goldwyn-Mayer
Irene Rich—Independent
Dorothy Sebastian—Metro-Goldwyn-Mayer
Virginia Valli—Independent

RED-HEADS
Mary Astor—Fox
Sally Eilers—Mack Sennett-Pathé
Merna Kennedy—Universal
Jacqueline Logan—Pathé
Audrey Ferris—Warner Brothers
Margaret Livingston—Columbia
Myrna Loy—Warner Brothers
Blanche Mehaffey—Independent

BROWN HAIR
Betty Bronson—Warner Brothers
Sue Carol—Independent
Betty Compson—Independent
Doris Kenyon—Independent
Patsy Ruth Miller—Independent
Mary Philbin—Universal

And many, many other lovely stars

RED-HEADS

Clara Bow, Paramount— "Lux Toilet Soap helps keep the skin in perfect condition."

Joan Crawford, M. G. M. —"Lux Toilet Soap is lovely for keeping my skin fresh and smooth."

Nancy Carroll, Paramount —"Lux Toilet Soap helps keep one's skin so flawless for the camera."

Janet Gaynor, Fox star, says: "Lux Toilet Soap makes my skin feel so soft and smooth."

BROWN HAIR

Evelyn Brent, Paramount —"Lux Toilet Soap is so delightfully pleasing and soothing."

Renée Adorée, M. G. M. —"Lux Toilet Soap gives my skin such a beautiful smoothness."

Mary Brian, Paramount —"Lux Toilet Soap is lovely for keeping one's skin in perfect condition."

Eleanor Boardman says: "It is excellent for the very smooth skin a screen star must have."

LUX Toilet Soap

Luxury such as you have found only in French soaps at 50c and $1.00 the cake . . . Now **10¢**

The Record Breaking

FAIRFORM
FLYER

56' Fairform Flyer, built by Huckins Yacht Corp., Jacksonville, Fla. Equipped with twin Dolphin Special 6 cylinder Sterling engines 290 H. P. each, 1950 R. P. M.

Modern in design and speed, equipped with established seasoned engines, the new Fairform Flyer suggests a late afternoon cruise—the antithesis of the lawn party of the 'eighties. Or, perhaps a week end journey of exploration—new scenery, open space, relaxation, and kindred terms, that prepare you for Monday with a feeling of having rediscovered America. .   .   .   .

STERLING ENGINE COMPANY
BUFFALO, NEW YORK, U. S. A.

Fairform Flyer. Ad. Douglas Donald. 1930. Sterling Engine Company

Lux Toilet Soap. Ad. 1929. Lever Brothers Limited

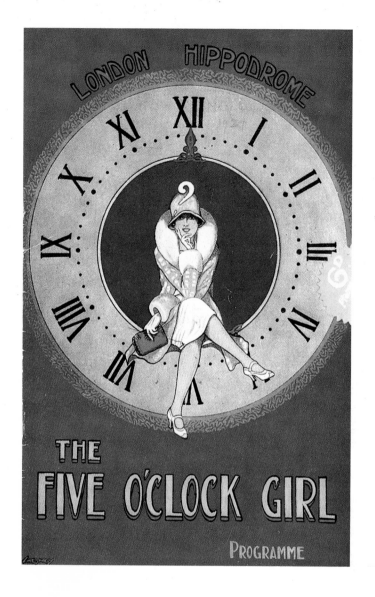

Life magazine. Cover. John Held, Jr. 1928.
Life Publishing Co.

The Five O'Clock Girl, musical comedy. Programme
cover. Paul Chesney. 1929. London Hippodrome

Good News, musical comedy. Ad. Aubrey Hammond. 1928.
Carlton Theatre, London

Vanity Fair magazine. Cover. Fish (Anne Harriet Fish). 1923. The Condé Nast Publications Inc.

BY APPOINTMENT TO H. R. H.
THE PRINCE OF WALES

Complexions that keep the first fair bloom of youth

GIVE YOUR SKIN THE SAME LOVELINESS THAT HAS MADE ENGLISH BEAUTY FAMOUS

PERHAPS there is no lovelier thing in all this world than the English girl at the age when she makes her curtsey to Their Majesties. There is an eagerness about her, a vibrancy and a freshness that no later time will ever quite recapture.

But her complexion, pink and white as porcelain, delicate and fine, is proof against the unkind years. Like eight generations of beautiful women before her, she will protect it with the finest toilet preparations she can buy. They will be Yardley's, from that London perfume house famous since 1770 for its English Lavender, and all of them are now available to you.

Yardley's English Lavender Soap, known as the Luxury Soap of the world, will guard the clear beauty of the most sensitive skin. It is so cooling and refreshing, so fragrant that it may be used as often during the day as you like.

Yardley's English Complexion Cream is the only cream you will need to keep your skin as soft and lovely as a child's. It is cleansing agent, skin food and powder foundation, all in one. Use it after your soap and water cleansing to penetrate the pores and free them of all disfiguring impurities. Use it at night as a nourishing cream to rebuild the relaxed tissues; and in the morning as a base for Yardley's English Lavender Face Powder . . . a filmy powder, light as chiffon, made in six subtle skin-tones.

Here in these three Yardley preparations you have the entire secret of English beauty. And if you would like to know about other Lavender toiletries, write for our free booklet, "Complexions with an English Accent." Yardley & Co., Ltd., 452 Fifth Avenue, New York City; in London, at 33 Old Bond Street; also Toronto and Paris.

Photograph by Eric Gray, London

YARDLEY'S English Complexion Cream, to cleanse, nourish and protect your skin. It is also used as a powder foundation, and can be washed away with water. $1.50. Yardley's English Lavender Face Powder in six skilfully blended shades. $1. Yardley's English Lavender Soap for complexion and bath. Bland, cooling, refreshing. Box of 3 cakes, $1, or 35c a cake. Bath size, 50c. Guest size, 6 in a box, $1, or 20c singly.

YARDLEY'S ENGLISH LAVENDER

YOUTH, all eagerness and vibrancy, should have a special perfume of its own . . . not the heavy bouquet or the exotic oriental flower. These would be as out of place for the debutante as the rope of pearls her mother might wear. But there is a fragrance that seems created just to express the fresh, sweet charm of youth. Yardley's English Lavender, delicate, winsome, lovable, has never had a rival in the English girl's affections. She uses it, as eight generations of her family have used it, in every personal appointment. In its wistful fragrance is caught something of that eternal, questing spirit which is recognized the world around as the attribute, the inalienable right, of youth. Yardley's English Lavender Perfume may be had in bottles of various sizes, ranging in price from $15 to $1.

YARDLEY'S ENGLISH LAVENDER . . . THE SWEET, COOL, WINSOME FRAGRANCE THAT YOUTH HAS ALWAYS LOVED

Yardley's English Lavender fragrance. Ad. Eric Gray. 1931. Yardley & Co., Ltd

As Madonna more stirringly Beautiful than *nine years ago* .. Lady Diana Manners says
"I depend entirely on the creams I chose then"

In 1924

Lady Diana Manners, when she first appeared in "The Miracle."
Famed as the most beautiful woman of English aristocracy,
Lady Diana said: "I know that every woman can effectively
accomplish loveliness by using Pond's Two Creams."

Today

Loving audiences are again spellbound by the still beauty,
more moving than ever, of Lady Diana Manners, now
Lady Diana Duff-Cooper, as she plays the famous rôle of
Madonna in the recent London revival of "The Miracle."

"CONTRARY to common belief, women on the stage seek the simplest methods to care for the skin." Lady Diana Duff-Cooper speaks with disarming British candor.

"After all," she declares, "good care of your skin consists only in cleansing it thoroughly with a pure cream, and *always* protecting it."

That surprises you. As you look at the exquisite loveliness of Lady Diana's complexion, you imagine that she uses many secret and expensive formulas for beauty.

Uses Just Two Creams

"It was in America when I first opened in 'The Miracle' that I discovered Pond's Two Creams. From that time on I have been positively devoted to them.

"I use Pond's Cold Cream *constantly* (day and night and always after exposure) to cleanse my skin—and it removes make-up perfectly! Also when one's face feels tired a generous patting of Pond's Cold Cream revives and stimulates it.

"And the Vanishing Cream is a hope fulfilled. I should feel lost without it! It is such a glorious foundation for cosmetics. And never do I expose my skin in any climate without first smoothing it on. It is the most enchanting, most protective cream I have ever known. I am always preaching its wonderful efficacy."

Lady Diana Manners adds: "I am delighted with Pond's new Face Powder. Almost unbelievable . . . so exquisite a powder at so moderate a price!"

Lady Diana Manners uses Pond's Cold Cream —"To cleanse the skin thoroughly of all foreign particles after every exposure.

"To remove all traces of cosmetics from face and lips."

She uses Pond's Vanishing Cream: "Always as a foundation for make-up. It's simply perfect and holds the powder like nothing else.

"Before every sport and every exposure.

"To smooth chapped and roughened skin if I have been careless.

"Almost every day to keep my hands and arms soft and white."

Pond's Famous Creams and New Face Powder

Many titled Englishwomen use and praise Pond's simple way to beauty. Among them:
The Marchioness of Carisbrooke
The Lady Louis Mountbatten
The Countess Howe
The Lady Violet Astor
Lady Georgiana Curzon

Send 10¢ (to cover cost of postage and packing) for choice of free samples

POND'S EXTRACT COMPANY, Dept. D
107 Hudson Street . . . . . . New York City
Please send me (check choice): *Pond's New Face Powder* in attractive jar. Light Cream □; Rose Cream □; Brunette □; Naturelle □.
OR *Pond's Two Creams, Tissues and Freshener* □.

Name_____

Street_____

City_____State_____
Copyright, 1933, Pond's Extract Company

TUNE IN on Pond's program every Friday, 9:30 P. M., E. S. T. . . . Leo Reisman and his Orchestra . . . WEAF and NBC Network

Pond's, face cream and powder. Ad. © 1933. Pond's Extract Company

Royal Palace Hotel, London. Menu cover. Victor Reinganum.
1932. J. Lyons & Co., Ltd

Biarritz magazine. Circular (detail). Hemjic.
c. 1930. Georges Gautron, Editeur

Cocktail. Menu cover. T. M. D. 1930. Grand Hotel, Stockholm

The matchless quality of Schweppes Table Waters makes them the accepted Standard of Good Taste.

Schweppes Table Waters. Ad. F. S. May. 1931. Schweppes Co., Ltd

"Thus off they went, and four-in-hand
Dash'd briskly tow'rds the promis'd land."

To-day in comfort by "Green Line" Coach

Le roman de Marguerite Gautier (Camille), motion picture. Poster. 1937. Metro-Goldwyn-Mayer

'Green Line', motor coach tours. Poster. Jean Dupas. 1933. London Passenger Transport Board.

Black Cat cigarettes. Calendar (Sylvia Whale). c. 1930.
Carreras Ltd

Player's Navy Cut cigarettes. Ad. 1931.
The Imperial Tobacco Company, Ltd

Wills's 'Gold Flake' cigarettes. Ad. Douglas Wales. 1930.
W. D. &. H. O. Wills Ltd

GOOD.. they've got to be good!

Fred and Adele Astaire in Broadway's musical hit, "The Band Wagon"

Darn good—you'll say!

Everybody wants a mild cigarette. And when you find one that is milder and *tastes better* too—you've got a smoke! Chesterfields are so much milder that you can smoke as many as you like. Mild, ripe, sweet-tasting tobaccos — the best that money can buy. That's what it takes to make a cigarette as good as Chesterfield. And the *purest* cigarette paper!

Every Chesterfield is well-filled. Burns evenly. Smokes cool and comfortable. *They Satisfy* sums it all up!

EVERYBODY'S GETTING ON "THE BAND WAGON"

© 1931, LIGGETT & MYERS TOBACCO CO.

Chesterfield cigarettes. Ad. c. 1931. Liggett & Myers Tobacco Co

Harrods, department store. Ad. 1936.
Harrods Ltd, London

Henri Bendel, fashion store. Ad. Forbath & Rejane
(at the Metropolitan Opera House). 1935.
Henri Bendel Inc, New York

Bergdorf Goodman, fashion store. Ad (Gladys George).
Alfredo Valente. 1935. Bergdorf Goodman Inc, New York

Nights in June

Glamorous nights of dancing and gaiety following upon days spent dashing round the town . . . . The pace is set for the young and eager but you can dance till dawn and succumb to the temptations of the most talented chef with never a worry about face or figure. *There is always tomorrow at Elizabeth Arden's.* An hour's treatment with the lovely Velva Cream Masque will relax your nerves and refresh your spirit. You will emerge looking your beautiful best in anticipation of another gala evening. Before you leave, ask your assistant to let you try Miss Arden's new perfume "Night and Day," so exactly right for lovely clothes, and grand occasions. You simply must wear it with that new frock with its masses of tulle and flowers.

Ardena Reducing Baths not only melt away the pounds but free your system of poisons and permit you to relax completely, gloriously, the while your reducing is being done for you. A body massage afterwards completes your feeling of being "on top of the world."

Elizabeth Arden

Elizabeth Arden Ltd

LONDON 25 OLD BOND STREET W1

Elizabeth Arden, salon and beauty products. Ad. After Baron de Meyer. 1936. Elizabeth Arden, Ltd

Moss Bros: General Outfitters. Ad. H. M. Bateman. 1935. Moss Bros & Co Ltd

Stage magazine. Cover (Leslie Howard). 1935.
Stage Magazine

Theatre: go by Underground. Poster. Barnett Freedman. 1936.
London Passenger Transport Board

The Scarlet Empress, motion picture. Poster (Marlene Dietrich).
1934. Columbia-Warner

Hotel St. Regis: Maisonette Russe. Ad (detail). Bobri
(Vladimir Bobritsky). 1939. Hotel St. Regis, New York

The Play Pictorial magazine. Cover (Noel Coward and
Gertrude Lawrence). 1930. The Play Pictorial

Airflow De Soto. Ad. Martin Munkacsi. 1935.
Chrysler Corporation

LEFT:
Cannon Towels. Ad. Herbert Matter. 1939. Cannon Mills Inc

OPPOSITE:
Matson-Oceanic liners. Ad. Edward Steichen. 1934.
Matson Line-Oceanic Line

Austin Reed's, men's clothing shop. Ad. Austin Cooper. 1930. Austin Reed Ltd, London

STEICHEN

Dining Saloon S. S. Lurline—Photograph taken enroute to Hawaii.

Hawaii

S. S. LURLINE • S. S. MARIPOSA
S. S. MONTEREY • S. S. MALOLO

Booklets full of ideas free at your travel agency, or

Matson Line • Oceanic Line

All the good things of life are on their native soil in Hawaii. You sample them in generous measure on Matson-Oceanic liners—palatial new ships inspired by the Islands they serve. At your command a whole cargo of clever devices for your entertainment and comfort.

Your only duty . . . go anywhere and do anything . . . whenever you wish. Sounds like a millionaire's idea of a vacation . . .

and *is.* But all the happy people sailing to Hawaii are not millionaires. Just people who know where to get the most for their time and money. *It's only a 5-day sail to the Islands from California.*

The inspiration of these magic regions invite you to continue through the South Seas. *Only 15 days to New Zealand from California. To Australia . . . only 18!* Via Hawaii, Samoa, Fiji. *At modest fares.*

New York, 535 Fifth Ave. • Chicago, 230 North Michigan Ave. • San Francisco, 215 Market Street • Los Angeles, 730 South Broadway • Seattle, 814 Second Ave. • Portland, 327 Southwest Pine Street

Mayfair hotel, London. Ad. Eric Fraser. 1930. Gordon Hotels Ltd

Punch magazine. Cover (based on Richard Doyle's 1885
design). 1935. Bradbury, Agnew & Co., Ltd

A Coach for Cinderella. Ad (detail). John C. Atherton.
1932. Fisher Body Corporation

Fortnum and Mason's, food delicacies. Catalogue cover. After Rex Whistler. 1938. Fortnum & Mason Ltd

IM TAKING AN
EARLY HOLIDAY COS
i KNOW SUMMER
COMES SOONEST IN THE SOUTH
SOUTHERN RAILWAY

Good Travelling Companions

THE
Leaves
PUBLISHED BY THE LONDON & NORTH EASTERN RAILWAY

'I'm taking an early holiday cos . . .' Poster.
Charles E. Brown. 1936. Southern Railway Company

Good Travelling Companions. Ad. 1935.
Illustrated Newspapers Ltd

The Night Scotsman. Ad. Alexeieff. 1932. London & North-Eastern Railway

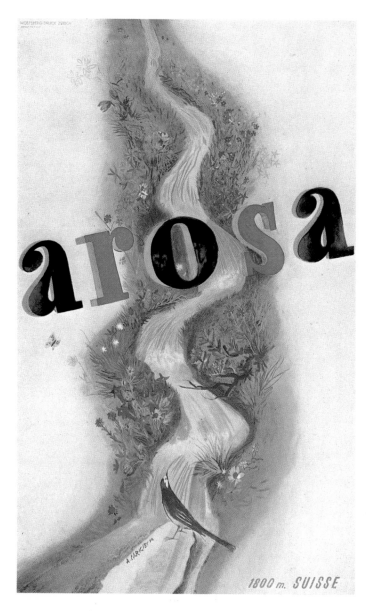

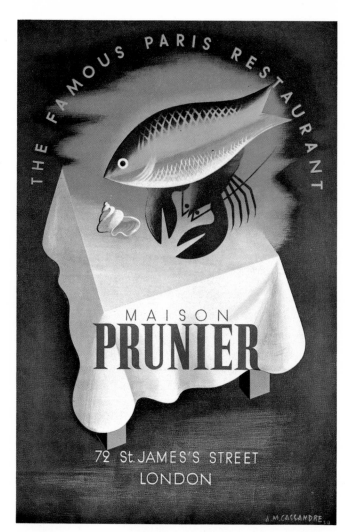

Arosa. Poster. Alois Carigiet. 1939. Swiss Travel Bureau

TOP RIGHT:
Maison Prunier, restaurant. Poster. A. M. Cassandre
(Adolphe Jean-Marie Mouron). 1935. Maison Prunier, London

RIGHT:
Sweepstakes: Prix de L'Arc de Triomphe. Poster.
A. M. Cassandre. 1935. Longchamp Racetrack

Angleterre: 'horses and elm trees at high noon'. Poster. A. M. Cassandre. 1934. British Railway Companies

Normandie, transatlantic liner. Poster. A. M. Cassandre. 1935. French Lines

Watney's Brown Ale. Display card. Edwin Calligan. 1937.
Watney, Combe, Reid & Co., Ltd

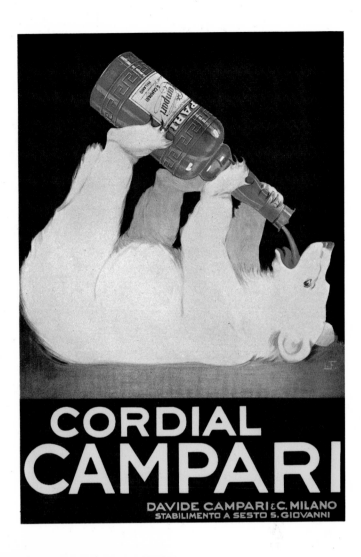

Cordial Campari. Poster. F. Laskoff. 1938.
Davide Campari & Co

Dubo . . . Dubon . . . Dubonnet. Poster.
A. M. Cassandre. 1937. Dubonnet

Shell petroleum. Poster. John Reynolds. 1930.
Shell-Mex Ltd

BP Ethyl petroleum. Poster. Tom Purvis. 1935.
British Petroleum Co., Ltd

—That was!

JOHN REYNOLDS

National Benzole mixture. Poster. Dronsfield.
1937. National Benzole Co., Ltd

parfum poudre rouge a lèvres made in france

Shocking de Schiaparelli. Ad. Marcel Vertes. 1937. Parfums Schiaparelli Inc

Basil's Ballets Russes. Programme cover. Christian Bérard. 1937. Colonel W. de Basil's Ballets Russes de Monte-Carlo, Théâtre des Champs-Elysées

Allwheat Crispbread. Ad (detail). Rico le Brun. c. 1933.
Peek Frean & Co., Ltd

Simpson's men's clothing shop. Ad. Hof. 1937.
S. Simpson, Ltd, London

Jaeger Greys, woolens. Ad. Francis Marshall. 1939.
Jaeger Co., Ltd

Die Dame magazine. Circular (detail). Alice Bronsch. 1938. Ullstein Verlag

THERE'S ABSOLUTELY NO LIMIT
TO WHAT YOU CAN PUT ON A HORSE
IF YOU —

Tell "Duggie" all about it!

—he's waiting to open a Credit Account with you

DOUGLAS STUART · STUART HOUSE · SHAFTESBURY AVE · LONDON

Douglas Stuart, turf accountant. Ad. W. Heath Robinson.
1936. Douglas Stuart, Ltd

*Have a glass of Guinness
when you're Tired*

Guinness beer. Ad. H. M. Bateman. 1938.
Arthur Guinness, Son & Co., Ltd

Perfect Circle, piston rings. Ad (detail). Tony Sarg.
1934. The Perfect Circle Company

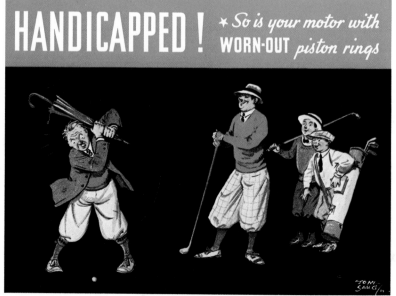

HANDICAPPED ! *So is your motor with* WORN-OUT *piston rings*

My Goodness, My Guinness. Poster. John Gilroy. 1938. Arthur Guinness, Son & Co., Ltd

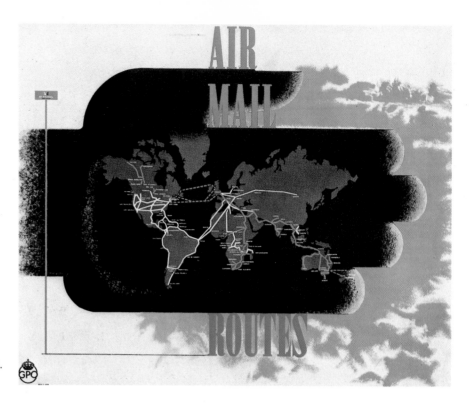

Air Mail Routes. Poster. E. McKnight Kauffer. 1937.
General Post Office

Imperial Airways. Ad. 1935. Imperial Airways Ltd

New York World's Fair. Poster. Joseph Binder. 1939.
New York World's Fair Corporation

South America in 3 days and nights! Poster. J. Wiertz. c. 1935. Deutsche Zeppelin-Reederei

Poster for disarmament. Jean Carlu. 1932.
Propaganda Office for Peace, Paris.

Rifle competition. Poster. Rudolf Lipus. 1934.
Leipzig Rifle Association

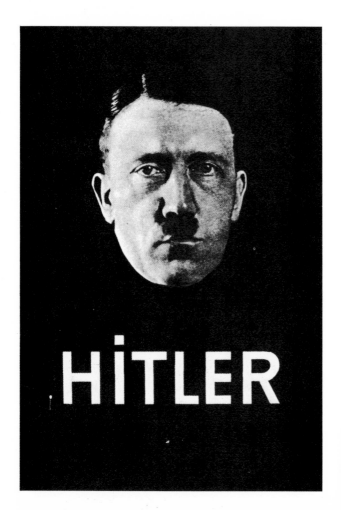

German election poster. 1932. The Nazi Party

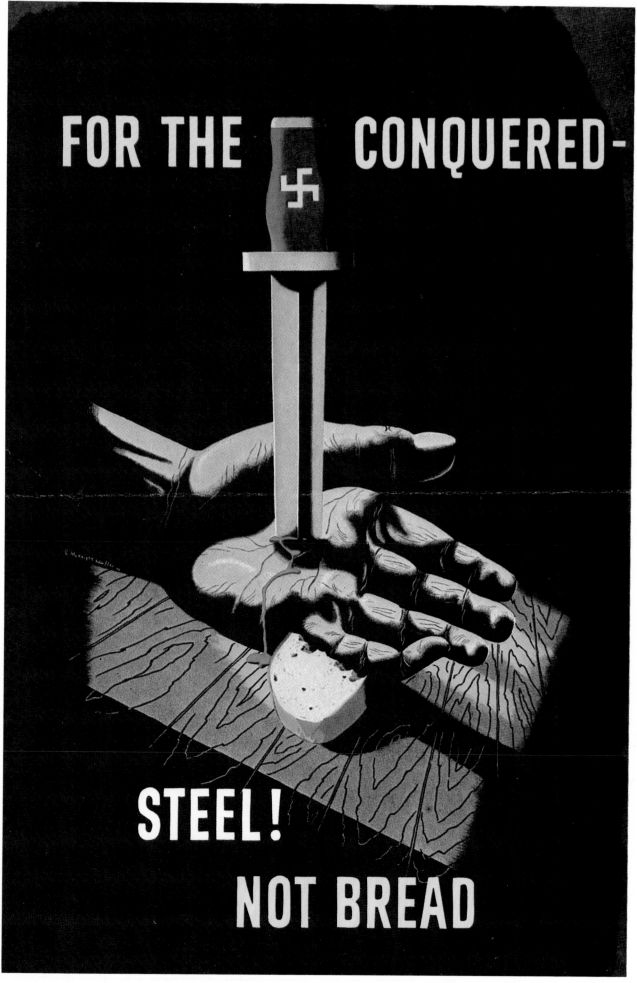

Anti-Nazi propaganda poster. E. McKnight Kauffer. c. 1940

1940-1960

New Year's Day 1940 was one of the bleakest in England's history. In 1938 Prime Minister Chamberlain's efforts to preserve 'peace with honour', which split the country politically, had at least gained Britain time to be better prepared for the inevitable showdown with Hitler (page 148). In 1939 Nazi Germany and Mussolini's Italy controlled most of Europe; and Hitler, on his way to grabbing the rest of it, marched into Poland—which was one goose step too far.

Still relatively unarmed, England, joined by France, declared war on Germany, and with a stiff upper lip London prepared to resist the beating Hitler promised to give it from the air. Before the sirens began to wail, Churchill (page 157) was in command, and through the fears and perils following the fall of France and the evacuation at Dunkirk he led England through its 'finest hour', the Battle of Britain, to victory and the German surrender on May 8, 1945.

The course of war had changed radically in 1941 when Hitler invaded Russia and Japan bombed Pearl Harbor. America's supporting role as 'the arsenal of democracy' immediately changed; her answer was no longer just 'production' (page 157) but war.

In 1944, as President Roosevelt's unprecedented third term drew to a close, F. D. R. announced he would run for a fourth. But two months after conferring with Churchill and Stalin at Yalta on ways to end the war, he died on April 12, 1945, and was succeeded by Harry S Truman. In August, when Japan refused to surrender, A-bombs were dropped on civilians on Hiroshima and Nagasaki, and a stunned and horrified world prayed that nothing like it would ever happen again. The basic power of the universe had been harnessed, and the Age of the Atom had begun.

The war had occupied half the decade, and in July 1945, Churchill's Conservatives were defeated by Clement Atlee's Labour Party, which began implementing its 'welfare state' promises by nationalizing the Bank of England, the railways, the coal, steel, and gas industries, and the airlines, which now advertised regular passenger service across oceans as well as continents. Free medical care soon followed, as did government patronage of the arts.

Meanwhile a tired, impoverished country tidied up its war-torn streets and tended to its bomb-damaged monuments. America's funds for rebuilding a strong democratic Europe helped, and when the pound was devalued, Britain's exports perked up.

In America it became a Trumanism to say that the New Deal had become a Fair Deal, especially for the ten million war veterans who, returning to civilian life, were aided by government services, loans and subsidized education. Wives and sweethearts had wartime savings to spend and tired of being a uniformed WAC, WAVE, WREN, or 'Rosie the Riveter', took happily to the Christian Dior-inspired New Look (page 194), a last love affair with elegance before fashion got the 'sack'.

Pin-ups of Betty Grable, Rita Hayworth (page 221), and the Petty Girl (161) were left behind as servicemen came home to the real thing. Marriage and babies added to the general postwar boom, and the bobby-soxer baby-sitter became a permanent institution. The latest teenage croon king was Frank Sinatra, rivalled only by Bing Crosby (page 176), whose singing of Irving Berlin's 'White Christmas' had already snowballed him to fame.

It was in 1943 that Broadway woke to 'Oh, What a Beautiful Morning' as *Oklahoma!*, a new kind of musical comedy, opened at the St. James. Out had gone the high-kicking chorus line and in had danced Agnes de Mille. Ballet sequences, like the songs, had become an integral part of the play. After the death of Lorenz Hart, Richard Rodgers teamed with Oscar Hammerstein, and the two continued to collaborate on a string of rousing successes, including *South Pacific*—with Enzio Pinza and Mary Martin (page 200)—*The King and I*, and, in 1959, *The Sound of Music*. Meanwhile, in 1956, Alan J. Lerner and Frederick Loewe had set Bernard Shaw's *Pygmalion* to music and made history with Rex Harrison and Julie Andrews in *My Fair Lady* and again in the 1964 film version with Audrey Hepburn in the role of Eliza (page 246).

The population explosion saw the masses spreading outward from the cities. Rows and rows of bungalow-type ranch houses were built for young families, and retirement communities for the old. As developers felled trees, a new kind of forest sprouted on rooftops—the antennae of TVs.

With the popularity of television, a wincing movie industry saw the closing of hundreds of movie houses, but producers, by making full use of new processes, the new wide screen, colour, and box-office stars like Bette Davis, Humphrey Bogart, Ingrid Bergman (page 193), Gary Cooper, Katharine Hepburn, Bob

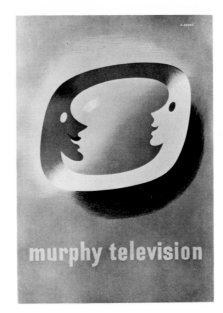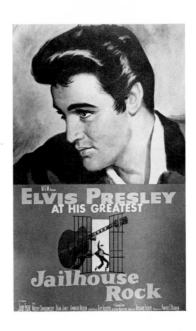

Hope (page 176), Danny Kaye (page 177), and Marilyn Monroe, who became the sex-symbol legend of the fifties (page 216), kept it alive if not always kicking. The industry also made money by producing for television as well as renting out old films.

Book publishers also feared the leisure-time competition of television, but name novelists like James A. Michener, Frank Yerby, Ernest Hemingway, Daphne DuMaurier kept selling, as did Lloyd C. Douglas, Thomas Wolfe, William Faulkner, and Thomas Costain. Paperbacks were also highly profitable.

In keeping with the times, advertising changed from the punchy, patriotic war ad to lightness and delicacy, as typified in the work of Salvador Dali, Raoul Dufy, and René Gruau. Distinguished avant garde work was being done by George Giusti for *Fortune* and *Holiday;* by Paul Rand, Joseph Binder, Ashley Havinden, and F. H. K. Henrion. Popular magazine-type illustration was well represented in the designs of artists like Jon Whitcomb, Whitney Darrow, Peter Hawley, Tom Hall, Jack Welch, and Norman Rockwell; and humour, never long absent in advertising, in the drawings of Fougasse, Raymond Tooby, Ronald Searle, Peter Arno, Richard Taylor, Robert Day, William Steig, and James Thurber. Photographers much in the fore included Cecil Beaton, Horst, Irving Penn, Francesco Scavullo, Yousuf Karsh, John Rawlings, and Leslie Gill—all represented in the following pages.

The theatre had seldom been stronger. In 1940 Ethel Barrymore had the best part of her career as Miss Moffat in Emlyn Williams' *The Corn Is Green,* the role created by Sybil Thorndike earlier in London. Lillian Hellman wrote *Watch on the Rhine*—and later *The Little Foxes,* which starred Tallulah Bankhead—John Van Druten *The Voice of the Turtle,* Thornton Wilder *The Skin of Our Teeth.* The Old Vic had a vigorous cast headed by Laurence Olivier, Ralph Richardson, and Margaret Leighton, playing to packed houses in 1946. In 1945 an unknown, Tennessee Williams, hit the jackpot with *The Glass Menagerie,* starring Laurette Taylor, and again in 1947 with *A Streetcar Named Desire,* pitting young Marlon Brando, a tough guy in a torn T-shirt, against Jessica Tandy onstage, and later against Vivien Leigh in the 1951 film version. In 1948 Henry Fonda was *Mister Roberts,* and a year later came Arthur Miller's masterpiece *Death of a Salesman.*

The fifties, the decade of 'The Affluent Society', in which author John Kenneth Galbraith called attention to the problems of abundance, saw war-hero Dwight Eisenhower, the advocate of 'fiscal responsibility', President of the United States for all but two years of it.

In England Churchill and the Conservatives came back in power the year of the 'Festival of Britain', which celebrated the hundredth anniversary of the Great Exhibition of 1851. A year later the sadness at the death of King George VI was replaced by the joy of a new coronation and a young Queen Elizabeth II. In 1956 another royal affair found Grace Kelly, recently opposite James Stewart in Hitchcock's *Rear Window* and with Cary Grant on the Riviera filming *To Catch a Thief,* returning to Monaco to become Princess Grace.

The fifties was also the time of TV quiz shows like 'What's My Line?' and for little boys to be coon-capped Crocketts or Boones.

Then suddenly, as parents might be listening to Julie Andrews singing 'I Could Have Danced All Night' or a smooth Harry Belafonte or Perry Como, a new kind of sound arose from across the Tennessee hills—Elvis Presley with his electric guitar, singing 'Don't Be Cruel'. The rock-'n'-roll heat wave coincided with the 'beat' movement fanning east out of San Francisco. Sultry, leather-jacketed youths living in pads and on pot hung around the streets, identifying with characters such as *The Wild One* in Marlon Brando's film and the moody and intense *Rebel Without a Cause* in James Dean's; with Allen Ginsberg's 'Howl', John Osborne's *Look Back in Anger,* and Jack Kerouac's *On the Road.* These were the first rumblings of the cultural earthquake that shook the sixties.

FROM LEFT TO RIGHT:

Holding the Line! Poster by Henri Guignon. c. 1942

Poster for Rodgers and Hammerstein's *Oklahoma!* by Hilary Knight. 1943

'We will control atomic energy, or it will control us.' From an ad for Scripps-Howard Newspapers. 1946

Ad for Lord & Taylor store by Dorothy Hood. 1952

Poster for Murphy Television by Abram Games. 1952

Poster for Elvis Presley's motion picture *Jailhouse Rock.* 1957

CARELESS TALK
COSTS LIVES

CARELESS TALK
COSTS LIVES

Defence posters. Fougasse (Cyril Kenneth Bird). 1940.
Ministry of Home Security, London

Blast the hub a

LOOK TO *Lockhee*

LOCKHEED AIRCRAFT CO

N FROM WALT DISNEY'S PRODUCTION,"VICTORY THROUGH AIRPOWER"

ash the wheel!

OR LEADERSHIP

BURBANK, CALIFORNIA

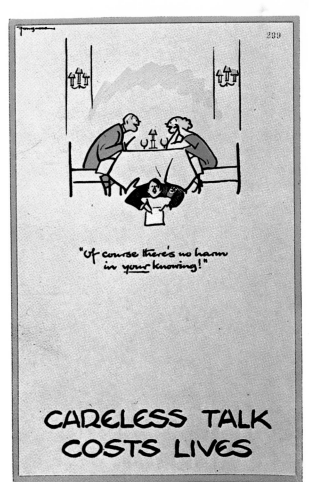

"Of course there's no harm in your knowing!"

CARELESS TALK
COSTS LIVES

".... strictly between these four walls!"

CARELESS TALK
COSTS LIVES

LEFT:
Lockheed. Ad. (Illustration from Walt Disney's production *Victory Through Airpower*). 1944. Lockheed Aircraft Corporation

Outposts of Britain. Poster.
E. McKnight Kauffer. 1940. General Post Office

Gateway Papers. Ad. 1941.
Wiggins Teape and Alex Pirie (Sales) Ltd

Save for the brave! Poster. A. Brener. 1941.
National Savings Committee

Answer Their Prayers. John Cook/Douglas Crockwell. c. 1942. American Relief for Holland Inc

Saving is Everybody's War Job. Poster. Tom Eckersley. 1943. Post Office Savings Bank of England

Deserve Victory! Poster (Winston Churchill). Little.
1941. Graham & Gillies Ltd

America's Answer! Production. Poster. Jean Carlu. 1942. Office for Emergency Management

"*PILOT TO WIFE...*"

Hello...

Hello...back there...

I know you won't get this message. It's only in my mind...but I've *got* to talk to you because there isn't much time. Here they come.

"Squadron leader to Fighting 4! Sixteen Zeros at 12 o'clock! Come on, you Hellcats! Here's what we've been looking for!"

Hello...back there...

We're out-numbered four to one today. Anything can happen. I know that. But this is *our* job, and it's got to be done.

I'm on my own and that's the way I like it ...but I'm not alone...we're all on the same team. Flying together, fighting together to win...not for ourselves but for each other...

For you...for home.

"Squadron leader to Fighting 4! All right, you guys...the sun's at our backs... let's get upstairs!"

Hello...back there...

Got to hurry now. But I want to tell you what I'm thinking about. I want to tell you what I'm fighting for...it's you and our little house and the job I had before...and the chance I had, the fighting chance, to go ahead on my own.

That's what all of us want out here...to win this war...to get home...to go back to being mechanics and storekeepers and salesmen and lawyers...and husbands and brothers and sons. To go back to living our lives in a land, and a world, where *every* man can be free to be somebody...where *every* man is free to grow as great as he's a mind to be...where every man has an *unlimited* opportunity to be useful to himself and to his fellow men.

"Squadron leader to Fighting 4! Okay! Let 'em have it!"

Hello...back there...

This is the payoff. Tell everybody...tell everybody back there...hello for me...

Tell 'em we'll be back...nothing can stop us...And tell 'em no matter what they say

...no matter what they do...to stay *free* ...to keep America a land of *individual* freedom!

That's what we're fighting for...

That's what we're willing to die for...

That's the America we want when we come home.

• • •

Here at Nash-Kelvinator we're building Pratt & Whitney engines for the Navy's Vought Corsairs and Grumman Hellcats...Hamilton Standard propellers for United Nations bombers... governors, binoculars, parts for ships, jeeps, tanks and trucks...readying production lines for Sikorsky helicopters. All of us devoted to winning this war... to speeding the peace when our men will come back to their jobs and homes and even better futures than they had before...to the day when together we'll build an even finer Kelvinator, an even greater Nash!

The Army-Navy "E" awarded to Nash-Kelvinator Corp., Propeller Division.

NASH-KELVINATOR CORPORATION
Kenosha · Milwaukee · DETROIT · Grand Rapids · Lansing

LET'S ALL BACK THE ATTACK!
BUY EXTRA WAR BONDS.

'Pilot to Wife . . .' Ad. Fred Ludekens. 1944. Nash-Kelvinator Corporation

© 1945 The Studebaker Corporation

"To the few to whom so many owe so much!"

Back the attack on all fronts with

WAR BONDS

Maybe you can't man a Studebaker Weasel but you can help our fighting forces by purchasing more and more U.S. War Bonds.

Awarded To All Studebaker Plants

THIS paraphrase of Winston Churchill's famous tribute to the Royal Air Force deservedly applies to all the men and women who wear our country's uniform.

A civilian grateful to all who have contributed to the success of the Flying Fortress addressed the sentiment to Studebaker some months ago. But it was really meant as an unreserved salute to every American fighting man on land, at sea and in the air.

Studebaker and its employees obviously are proud to have been called upon by our government to build the Cyclone engines that power the Boeing Flying Fortress—to produce huge quantities of Studebaker military trucks—to design and manufacture the versatile Studebaker Weasel personnel and cargo carrier.

But they are prouder still that they have been privileged throughout the war to put their willing hands to work in support of the efforts of the men and women in all branches of our nation's armed services.

Studebaker

PEACETIME BUILDER OF FINE CARS AND TRUCKS
WARTIME BUILDER OF WRIGHT CYCLONE ENGINES FOR BOEING FLYING FORTRESS

Also producing heavy-duty Studebaker military trucks and Weasel personnel and cargo carriers

Studebaker cars and Wright Cyclone engines. Ad. Frederick Hollander. © 1945. The Studebaker Corporation

Capehart, phonograph-radio. Ad. William Gropper. 1943.
Farnsworth Television & Radio Corporation

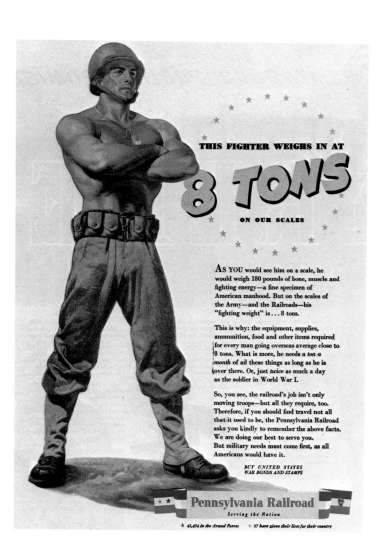

This Fighter Weighs in at 8 Tons. Ad. Frank J. Reilly. 1944.
Pennsylvania Railroad

Beauty and the Bomb . . . Ad. 1944. Shell Research Company

Buzzing with news *about Cigarettes!*

NEW "ZIP-TOP" PACK
Just pull
the tab . . . get 'em FRESH
in a FLASH! 2 Cellophane
jackets open with 1 zip!

Yes,
Betty Petty
Is keeping
The wires hot
But there's
Nothing phone-y
About this news . . .
Impartial tests *
Of 5
Leading brands
Of cigarettes
Now prove Old Gold
A truly *better*
Smoke . . .

PROVED FRESHEST

Of all 5 brands
In laboratory tests *
(Because of O.G.'s
Two jackets
Of Cellophane.)

WINS ON TASTE

With more smokers
Than any other brand
In Public Taste Tests. *
(Because fresher
Cigarettes
Do taste better.)
Why not get on
The receiving end
Of an Old Gold
Today?
We'll bet
You say
It rings the bell!

All tests conducted by unbiased independent research
authorities (names on request). *Economy Note:* The tests
proved Old Golds contain *more* tobacco by weight than
any of the other brands tested.

Old Golds . . . *FRESHEST* of all 5 . . . win on *TASTE!*

Old Golds. Ad. George Petty. © 1940. P. Lorillard & Co

PUBLIC NOTICE

'Tis the chief glory of the mighty to
be gracious, a prerogative of Kings
to conquer good-will.
...BALTASAR GRACIAN
Write Box 12, Wall St. Station, N.Y.C.

BALTASAR GRACIAN

LEJON
BRANDY
84 PROOF

Warm Greetings! Greetings of LEJON Brandy to you, sage of
Worldly Wisdom, Baltasar Gracian! Not Kings alone dispense
the glory of graciousness, but LEJON Brandy too. Did you not
once say: "Know how to choose well"?...Then for your better
choosing we dispatch to you a case of LEJON Brandy. Made
from choice grapes and tended by the wisdom of nature
and the vintner's love, it dispenses royal hospitality. The merest
taste will satisfy you of its might and conquering good-will.

LEJON

For Brandy Connoisseurs: We have a booklet, "The Spirit of the Grape".*
Write Dept. LG-15 Box 12, Wall St. Station, N. Y. C.
DISTRIBUTED BY NATIONAL DISTILLERS PRODUCTS CORPORATION, 120 BROADWAY, NEW YORK CITY
PRODUCED IN THE U. S. A.   *©1944   84 PROOF

Lejon Brandy. Ad. Lee Rackow. © 1944.
National Distillers Products Corporation

Plan ahead—the
ORIENT
—the world's supreme
travel experience!

Plan ahead for it now—
the Orient! It is bigger and
more beautiful and stranger
than other places in the world.
It is the temples and cities of
China, the friendship of the
Philippines, the tapestry of India
—all combined.
And now you can plan ahead
to reach it—in comfort—aboard
our new luxury liners.

NEW SHIPS FOR THE ORIENT
Backed by 75 years' inherited experience
in trans-Pacific service—our ships will
provide unprecedented comforts, gay
entertainment, swimming pools, shops.
Staterooms are: charming ship's-side
apartments by day—sumptuous bedrooms
by night. Complete with air-conditioning,
private bath, reading lamps, phone. All this
—plus wonderful food, courteous service,
carefree leisure! Yes, start planning now!

Normal 'Round-the-World service
touches 14 countries and 23 ports of call:
New York, Boston, Havana, Cristobal, Bal-
boa, Los Angeles, San Francisco, Honolulu,
Yokohama, Kobe, Shanghai, Hong Kong,
Manila, Singapore, Penang, Colombo,
Bombay, Suez, Port Said, Alexandria,
Naples, Genoa, Marseilles, (New York).

For details see your travel agent. Or write or
call on us at 604 Fifth Ave., New York 20;
177 State St., Boston 9; 716 Transportation
Bldg., Washington 6, D.C.; 110 South Dearborn
St., Chicago 3; 226 Henry Bldg., Seattle;
510 West Sixth St., Los Angeles 14; or 311
California St., San Francisco 4 (Head Office).

For 75 years America's link with the Orient.
AMERICAN PRESIDENT LINES

Plan *ahead*—the Orient. Ad. Al Camille. 1946.
American President Lines

Fred Allen says:

"SHIVER MY
TIMBERS!...

you wouldn't think a gallon
of FIRE-CHIEF gasoline
could go so far!"

You're welcome at
TEXACO DEALERS
There are more than 45,000
of us in all 48 States

TEXACO
T
REG.T.M.

TUNE IN FRED ALLEN every Sunday
night. See your local newspaper
for time and station.

Fire Chief gasoline. Ad (Fred Allen). 1942. Texaco Inc

There's plenty of
Old St. Croix at your
favorite store

86 Proof . . . General Distilleries Corp., Boston, Mass.

Old St. Croix rum. Ad. 'S'. 1943. General Distillers Corporation

THIS IS FOR KEEPS

Forsaking all others . . . *this is for keeps!* For keeps, too, and part of every girl's bridal dreams are her first home, the table for two, candlelight gracing softly gleaming Community.

For it is Community the bride puts high on her wishing list. She treasures the deep-etched distinction, the timeless good taste of Community patterns, the overlay of solid silver that protects each hard-wear point, Community's perfection of weight and balance. See the 50-piece service for eight places in a chest of polished beauty—at your jeweler's now . . . just $62.50. (No government tax.)

Community
THE FINEST SILVERPLATE

If its Community . . . its correct

CORONATION

LADY HAMILTON

MILADY

TRADE MARK   COPYRIGHT 1946 ONEIDA LTD.

Community silverplate. Ad. Jon Whitcomb. © 1946. Oneida Ltd

Ballantine's Ale. Ad. Carl Paulson/Fred Siebel. 1948. P. Ballantine & Sons

PM whiskey. Ad. Don Bender. 1946.
National Distillers Products Corporation

Easter shoes. Ad (detail). Bolin. 1946.
Brown Shoe Company

Naturalizer shoes. Ad. Constantin Alajalov. 1947.
Brown Shoe Company

Everybody knows the sign of good coffee

Who could resist such an invitation? To any true coffee lover it's a promise of *complete* coffee enjoyment ... of the truly "Good to the Last Drop" flavor that has made Maxwell House world-famous. And when refreshments are more officially served, this fragrant, flavor-rich coffee will meet with unanimous approval, for it is America's favorite— bought and enjoyed by more people than any other brand, *at any price!* Whenever, wherever, this tremendously popular coffee is served it is sure to please, for Maxwell House is *always* among friends.

TUNE IN . . . "Father Knows Best" . . . *delightful family comedy starring Robert Young . . . NBC, Thursday nights*

Now in Instant form too!

Instant MAXWELL HOUSE Coffee

MAXWELL HOUSE Coffee

Products of General Foods

Maxwell House . . . the <u>one</u> *coffee with that "Good to the Last Drop" flavor!*

Maxwell House Coffee. Ad. Helen E. Hokinson. 1949. General Foods Corp

Artist—William Traher, native of Wyoming

WYOMING—*annual purchases: $255 million—mostly packaged.*

CONTAINER CORPORATION OF AMERICA

Container Corporation of America. Ad. William Traher. 1949. Container Corporation of America

Toujours Moi perfume. Ad. Bobri. 1944. Parfums Corday Inc

toujours Moi

Toujours moi

CORDAY

bobri

Lily Daché hats. Ad (detail). Charles Kovec. 1949.
Frost Brothers

Disney, Hatmaker. Ad. Paul Rand. © 1947. Disney Inc

Tabu, the 'forbidden' fragrance. Ad. René Prinet. 1941.
Dana Perfumes Corp

A few pieces from the collection of costume jewelry by Nettie Rosenstein

Costume jewelry by Nettie Rosenstein. Ad. John Rawlings. 1946. Nettie Rosenstein

LEFT:

'Air-Spun' Makeup. Ad. Eric (Carl Erickson). 1944.
Coty Inc

ABOVE:

'Fatal Apple', face powder. Ad. Samberg. © 1946.
Revlon Products Corp

OPPOSITE LEFT:

Suchard chocolates. Box label. Albert Schneck. c. 1947.
Suchard, Neuchâtel

OPPOSITE RIGHT:

'Bond Street' by Yardley. Ad. Bernard Lamotte. 1947.
Yardley of London Inc

Double dare you to "taste" that new color

—"Fatal Apple"

Revlon

Creators of the world-famous nail enamel and lipstick.

It begins...much as other powders do...After all, certain pigments go into
all powder shades...**But it ends up** on your skin looking quite
different! Revlon custom-blending...that special Revlon talent for putting a
color "together"...results in face powder with new lift, new excitement...
to give you a dazzling, altogether new look! Try "Fatal Apple"...
color sensation created for the American woman of great chic...
Newest of eleven custom-made Revlon powder colors.

There's a language of loveliness that's understood the earth around—
the romantic, worldly fragrance of Yardley's "Bond Street,"
recalling beautiful faces and enchanting ways. It is the scent chosen by
women of sophistication, for it is as distinctive as they.
"Bond Street" Perfume, $2.50 to $15. Toilet Water, $1.50 and $2.50. Plus tax.

"Bond Street" **by YARDLEY**

Yardley products for America are created in England and finished in the U.S.A. from the original English formulae, combining imported and domestic ingredients. Yardley of London, Inc., 620 Fifth Avenue, N.Y.C.

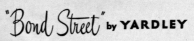

SUCHARD

SHE TOO IS WEARING A STETSON, THE GLOBE-TROTTER, $18.95. OTHER STETSON MILLINERY FASHIONS FROM $5.95.

Bing Crosby is currently starred in Paramount's "The Emperor Waltz."

Can't <u>both</u> be Bing Crosby!

They *are* both Bing Crosby, young lady. Not two *different people,* of course—but *the* Bing Crosby dressed for two different *occasions.* And that's the point of the picture: to show how simple it is to be well-dressed—by wearing the *right clothes* at the *right time.* Bing Crosby is one of Hollywood's best-dressed men. On

the left, he's dressed for travel, in the Stetson *Flagship,* Briar. On the right, he's ready for dinner in town, in the Stetson *Whippet.* Color: Sky Gray. You need neither fame nor fortune to be as well-dressed as Bing Crosby. Merely pick what you wear, carefully, to suit the occasion. Then top it off with the *right* Stetson.

Leaving the airport, Bing wears ...

The Stetson *Flagship,* $12.50

And meeting friends for dinner...

The Stetson *Whippet,* $10

Dress for the occasion with— STETSON HATS

More people wear Stetson Hats than any other brand. Stetson Hats are made only by John B. Stetson Company and its subsidiary companies in the United States and Canada.

"But, dear, mothers-in-law are harmless!"
cried Elsie

"THEY MAY BE HARMLESS," snorted Elmer, the bull, "but I'm not having any strange mothers-in-law cluttering up the place!"

"And nobody's asking you to, darling," smiled Elsie.

"Nobody ever asks me anything, not even Beulah!" fumed Elmer. "First off, I find a pair of strangers setting up housekeeping in my den! Next thing I know, the place will be alive with in-laws! Well, I'm getting out before they crawl in!"

"Now, calm down, sweet," soothed Elsie. "That young couple I rented your den to wouldn't have a place to rest their heads, if I hadn't taken them in. And we have more rooms than we need, so—"

"So you sacrificed my comfort," accused Elmer, "to get yourself an audience for your Borden prattle."

"Don't be silly, dear," smiled Elsie. "Young folks nowadays are born *hep* to the good things. Why, that little bride was telling *me*, Elsie, the Borden Cow, how to make 'but definitely' grand coffee in a jiffy with *Borden's Instant Coffee!*"

"Haw! Haw!" guffawed Elmer. "Someone beat you

Jiffy iced coffee—with Borden's Instant Coffee!

to the draw. Sounds like a smart young woman."

"Oh, she is!" agreed Elsie. "*She* says the 'de-vine' way to make iced coffee is with Borden's Instant—so easy and no waste."

"*That does it!*" exploded Elmer. "I'm not having *two* females tossing Borden's at me! I'm getting out!"

"Darling *dear*," soothed Elsie, "you know that the government has asked anyone who possibly can to put off buying or building a house right now."

"If the government's so smart," argued Elmer, "why didn't they see this housing shortage coming?"

"Even if they *did* see it," answered Elsie, "they had to go on using building materials for war. If you'll look back a few months, Elmer, you'll recall all kinds of shortages, including lots of wonderful Borden's foods."

"I haven't time for your Borden dance," snapped Elmer. "Gotta be on my way. But before I go, answer me this: How *long* are *they* going to camp in my den?"

"Only until they find the right house at the right price," answered Elsie. "Now, dear, if I promise to speed that day, will you *please* put away that funny-looking bundle?"

"We-ell," hesitated Elmer, "on one condition: *If I* stick around, everybody's gotta treat me as head man!"

"I'm glad you mentioned *treat*, dear," chirped Elsie, "because Borden's has the most scrumptious treat that ever brightened an ice-cream lover's heart. It's dreamy, peach-and-creamy *Borden's Fresh Peach Ice Cream.*"

"Who wants to eat a dream?" snorted Elmer. "Gimme

something you can spoon up and *taste!*"

"You'll *love* the taste of this ice cream," said Elsie.

Peach-and-creamy treat—
Borden's Fresh Peach Ice Cream!

"It's made with fresh, juicy peaches and real cream."

"*Aw!* Stop the sales chatter, woman," commanded Elmer, "and tell me is it any doggone *good?*"

"What a question!" giggled Elsie. "You know— *if it's Borden's, it's GOT to be good!*"

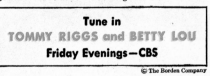

Tune in
TOMMY RIGGS and BETTY LOU
Friday Evenings—CBS

© The Borden Company

—if it's Borden's, it's got to be good!

Borden's, dairy products. Ad. E. V. Johnson. © 1946. The Borden Company

Stetson Hats. Ad. Clayton Underhill. 1948. John B. Stetson Company

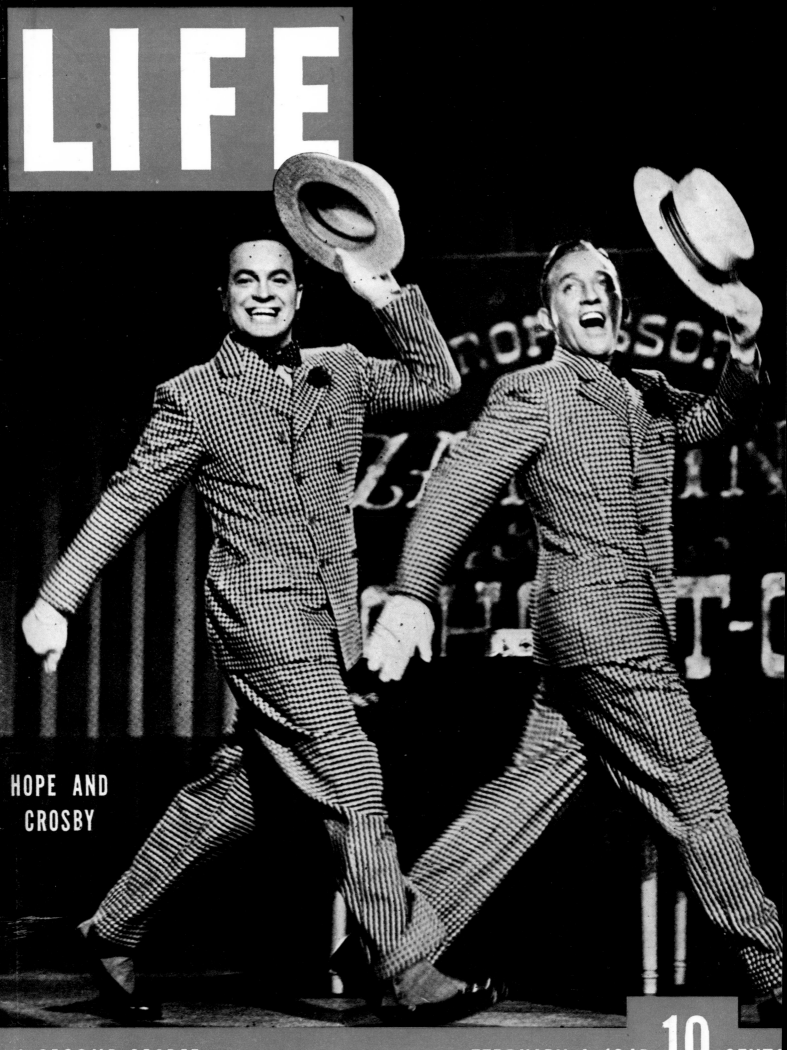

LIFE

HOPE AND
CROSBY

A SECOND SECRET
CHURCHILL SPEECH

FEBRUARY 4, 1946 **10** CENTS
YEARLY SUBSCRIPTION $4.50

REG. U. S. PAT. OFF.

All boats aren't Yachts!

All adhesive bandages aren't BAND-AID*

BAND-AID IS MADE ONLY BY *Johnson & Johnson*

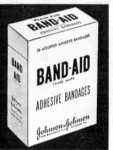

AND ONLY BAND-AID GIVES YOU JOHNSON & JOHNSON QUALITY!

It's Johnson & Johnson quality that has earned for BAND-AID Adhesive Bandages the confidence of millions.

More families use BAND-AID Adhesive Bandages—more doctors recommend them than any other brand.

Every bandage comes to you sterile, sealed in an individual envelope. Keeps out dirt; helps prevent infection, avoid irritation. Cost? Less than a penny each!

Keep one box at home—one at work.

*BAND-AID is the registered trade-mark of Johnson & Johnson for its adhesive bandage.

Are YOU a MITTY?

Can you, like Danny Kaye, daydream yourself as a daring ace? Can you become seven different personalities in your daydreams? Does the girl of your daydreams ever come true, like Virginia Mayo? How would you like to be frightened by **Boris Karloff**, hen-pecked by **Fay Bainter**, pursued by **Ann Rutherford**, and adored by the gorgeous **Goldwyn Girls**? You, too, can be a Mitty if you try! **Samuel Goldwyn**, who gave you "The Best Years Of Our Lives," now gives you *the best time of your life* in "**The Secret Life Of Walter Mitty**," photographed in Technicolor by Lee Garmes, directed by Norman McLeod and sparkling with matchless music.

"But I don't want to go home since you got rid of that "5 o'clock Shadow"!"

"By golly, I didn't know what life could be 'til I found out about Gem Blades!"

LET'S ALL BACK THE ATTACK — BUY WAR BONDS!

AVOID "5 O'CLOCK SHADOW" WITH

GEM
RAZORS and BLADES

© 1944, American Safety Razor Corp.

OPPOSITE:
Life magazine. Cover (Bob Hope and Bing Crosby). Jack Hoffman / Paramount Pictures. © 1946. Time Inc

LEFT:
Band-Aid, Adhesive Bandages. Ad. Richard Taylor. 1947. Johnson & Johnson

CENTER:
The Secret Life of Walter Mitty, motion picture. Ad (Danny Kaye and Virginia Mayo). Lee Garmes. 1947. Samuel Goldwyn Productions

RIGHT
Gem Razors and Blades. Ad. Peter Arno. © 1944. American Safety Razor Corp

Lastex yarn. Ad. John Cullen Murphy. 1948.
United States Rubber Company

Kotex Sanitary Napkins. Ad. Tom Hall. 1948.
West Chemical Products Inc

Irradiated Carnation Milk. Ad. 1944. Carnation Co

"First over the bars!"

Like a prize-winning jumper, Hunter has been developed slowly, expertly and with infinite care. For it takes *time*, *patience* and *skill* to produce a whiskey worthy of the acclaim that Hunter has received down through the years. And nothing less than eighty-six years of experience could have achieved the matchless flavor and the all-around excellence of today's Hunter— *An American Gentleman's Whiskey since 1860.*

HUNTER
FINE BLENDED WHISKEY

Hunter-Wilson Distilling Co., Inc., Louisville, Ky. Blended whiskey, 92 proof. The straight whiskies in this product are 6 or more years old. 40% straight whiskey. 60% grain neutral spirits.

Hunter Fine Blended Whiskey. Ad. George Shepherd. 1946. Hunter-Wilson Distilling Co., Inc

"That's what I call smart merchandising."

Pepsi-Cola beverage. Ad. Robert Day. 1947. Pepsi-Cola Co

Advertising bureau. Ad (detail). Fred Chance. 1947. The Bureau of
Advertising of the American Newspaper Association

RIGHT:
Lifebuoy soap. Ad. William Steig. 1944.
Lever Bros. Company

Talon fasteners. Ad (detail). James Thurber. 1941.
Talon, Inc

"So long, Junior. I warned you if you didn't
use Lifebuoy, I'd drop you from the act."

"I warned you" said the man on the flying trapeze. But in real life others don't tell you
when you have "B.O."—they merely avoid you. And *anyone* can offend because *everyone*
perspires, summer and winter. So do as careful millions do. Guard against offending by
using Lifebuoy in your daily bath—the only soap especially made to STOP "B.O."

Advertisement for steel (detail). Eric Fraser. 1949.
The United Steel Companies Ltd

Sundour, fine furnishing fabrics. Ad. Pearl Falconer. 1948.
Morton Sundour Fabrics Ltd

Acetate rayon fabric. Ad (detail). F. C. Harrison.
1949. British Celanese Ltd

Those Heavenly Carpets by Lees

*When you work out
your decorative scheme,
naturally you choose
fine carpet for the foundation.
And that brings you to a Lees—
for beautiful design,
resilient wool,
and color in the modern manner.
The carpet shown
is Skyline
in Tropical Green.*

Lees' carpets. Ad. Jan Balet. 1948. James Lees & Sons Company

What kind of music do you like best?

"The most popular man alive"—that's what Bing Crosby was voted in a recent nationwide poll! On his sparkling new variety show, Bing's at his tip-top best—and weekly guest stars include such favorites as Bob Hope, Jimmy Durante, Judy Garland (Wednesday, 10 p.m. EST. 9 p.m. in all other zones). (Philco.)

Music of the masters—brilliantly interpreted by masters of music! Don't miss conductor Karl Krueger and the magnificent 95-piece Detroit Symphony Orchestra in *The Sunday Evening Hour*—a series of uninterrupted full-hour broadcasts. Every Sunday evening, 8-9 p. m. EST. (Musical Digest.)

Grand Opera in all its breath-taking majesty! Every Saturday afternoon during the opera season, ABC invites you to thrill to the world's greatest opera stars, the world's most glorious music—direct from the stage of "the Met." Plus the stimulating entre-act features, *The Opera Quiz, Opera News on the Air,* and *The Opera Round Table* with famous guests participating. (Sponsored by The Texas Company.) Above: the noted Wagnerian tenor Lauritz Melchior in one of his greatest roles, as Tristan in *Tristan and Isolde*.

Kick back the rug and everybody dance to the "swing and sway" music of Sammy Kaye's popular orchestra. The inimitable Sammy broadcasts on *Sammy Kaye's Serenade* (Sunday, 1:30 p. m. EST) (Richard Hudnut) and on the lively *So You Want to Lead a Band* program (Monday, 9:30 p. m. EST).

Wonderful things happen when Inez Carillo and duo-pianists Cy Walter and Walter Gross play every Saturday (11:30 a. m. EST) on *Piano Playhouse*. Exciting music, celebrated guest stars and "that eminent musicologist" Dr. Milton Cross. (The scene above is all in fun, *not* a sample of the fine music you'll hear!)

Your all-time favorites are played in your favorite way by the "Dean of Modern American Music" himself, Paul Whiteman. The whole family will delight in the *Paul Whiteman Show*: popular melodies of yesterday and today, as only "Pops" can play them, and sung by leading soloists (Wednesday 9 p. m. EST).

You'll applaud great symphonic music every Tuesday evening (8:30—9:30 p.m. EST) when the world-famous Boston Symphony Orchestra broadcasts on ABC. Conducted by Dr. Serge Koussevitzky, this celebrated orchestra brings you the finest of the moderns as well as the masters. (The John Hancock.)

You shall have music ... the effortless, friendly voice of "Der Bingle" ... the melodious rhythm of Rex Maupin ... the breath-taking excitement of an aria by Lily Pons... the charm and gaiety of such musical treats as *Wake Up and Smile*, the *Music Library*, the *Johnny Thompson Show* and others. Yes, music on your local American Broadcasting Company station is music the way you like it ... music at its best.

Yet ABC does not deserve your attention for music alone. The network has outstanding programs of *every* type, in every field. Programs like the distinguished *Theatre Guild on the Air*; the deeply moving *Greatest Story Ever*

Told; the thrilling public service program *This Is Your FBI* and *Darts for Dough*, good fun for studio audience and listeners alike. Discover for yourself that there's *always* top-notch entertainment when you dial *your local ABC station.*

What makes a good network?

A network is known by the company it keeps: the calibre of its sponsors determines in great measure the calibre of its programs. ABC has its full share of top shows on the air because its roster of sponsors reads like a blue book of American industry. U. S. Steel, Equitable Life, Quaker Oats, Procter & Gamble, Goodyear, Miles Laboratories and Waterman Pens are only a few of the outstanding sponsors that are on ABC because they find the network is an effective and economical way of selling goods nationally.

Listen to
ABC American Broadcasting Company
A NETWORK OF 238 RADIO STATIONS SERVING AMERICA

Listen to ABC. Ad. 1947. American Broadcasting Company

Marian Anderson recording. Ad. Yousuf Karsh. 1944. RCA Victor Records

RAIT BY KARSH—OTTAWA

Marian Anderson evokes all the profound emotional power of Brahms'
"Alto Rhapsody" in a deeply expressive new recording

Recorded with the San Francisco Symphony Orchestra and
Municipal Chorus, Pierre Monteux, Conductor. Two Red
Seal Records in Showpiece SP-13. $2.25, exclusive of taxes.

E WORLD'S GREATEST ARTISTS ARE ON RCA VICTOR RECORDS

Lilliput magazine. Ad. Arpad Elfer. 1949.
Hulton Press Ltd

D. H. Evans, department store. Poster. Barbosa. 1945.
D. H. Evans & Co., Ltd, London

A & P Coffee. Poster. Joseph Binder. 1940.
American Coffee Corp

Graphis magazine. Cover. Joseph Binder. 1948. Amstutz & Herdeg, Zurich

If you're dragging yourself around

because the caffein in coffee interferes with your sleep...

switch to rich, delicious, caffein-free

Sanka Coffee

and sleep like this!

Sanka Coffee is superb coffee

All coffee—real coffee—finest coffee—97% caffein-free!

Drink it and sleep!

For your convenience, Sanka Coffee now comes in two delicious forms—New Instant Sanka, as well as your favorite grind for percolator or drip method!

A Product of General Foods

Sanka Coffee. Ad. c. 1947. General Foods Corp

makes the most of your best

A Cole swimsuit with Matletex*...designed to emphasize what you're proud to have...minimize what you wish you hadn't. Stock's still limited. To be sure, go to your nearest good store today.

*Cole's exclusive method of elasticizing for perfect fit.
*Reg. U.S. Pat. Off.

Cole, swim suits. Ad. 1947.
Cole of California, Inc

THE
Thinker

Here he sits. Thinking. Thinking why, oh why did he ever buy those pajamas without looking for the "Sanforized" trade-mark!

He knows, as well as he knows his wife's first name, that "Sanforized" means *permanent fit*. He knows "Sanforized" means a garment that will hold its *original comfort* till the cows come rambling home!

So he sits thinking that, from this day onward, he will *always* look for, demand, yell for, insist on seeing "Sanforized" on every label of every washable garment he buys!

("Sanforized" on the label means: fabric can't shrink more than a trifling 1%.)

The comfort never shrinks away from the garment with "Sanforized" on the label

•SANFORIZED•
TRADE ® MARK

Trade-Mark of Cluett, Peabody & Co., Inc.

The "Sanforized" trade-mark is used on compressive pre-shrunk fabrics only when tests for residual shrinkage are regularly checked by the owner of the trade-mark to insure maintenance of its established standard by users of the mark. *Cluett, Peabody & Co., Inc.*

'Sanforized', preshrunk fabrics. Leon Gregori. 1948. Cluett, Peabody & Co., Inc

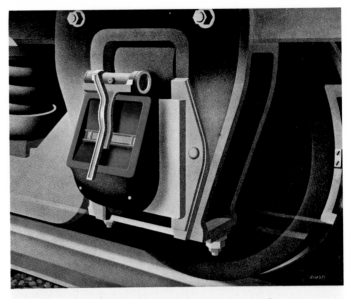

FAST TRAVELING PLASTICS!

THE ACCELERATED pace of fast-traveling plastics is carrying these useful materials still farther into the transportation field. Latest advance is a journal box cover molded from Ethocel, a Dow plastic development. Test runs show the new tightly fitting covers practically eliminate a principal cause of the "hot box"—an important forward step in maintaining vital train schedules. Moreover, this change to plastics saves from 30 to 50 pounds of steel per car.

Ethocel is used for this difficult plastic application because it possesses remarkable shock-resistance under extremes of high and low temperatures. At the same time, it is sufficiently flexible to permit the cover to "spring" into position, completely sealing the opening. Rain, dust, dirt and snow are thus kept out of the box that houses the axle bearings; oil is kept in. With this assurance of water-dry, clean and uninterrupted lubrication, "hot boxes" caused by lubrication failure are controlled. These are some of the reasons that place the new plastic plates in line with the continuous advance in railroad efficiency.

THE DOW CHEMICAL COMPANY, MIDLAND, MICHIGAN
New York · St. Louis · Chicago · San Francisco · Los Angeles · Seattle · Houston
Ethocel and Styron are registered Trade Marks

DOW
PLASTICS
Styron
Saran · Ethocel
Ethocel Sheeting
PRODUCTS OF CHEMICAL PROGRESS

Fast Traveling Plastics! Ad. George Giusti. 1942.
The Dow Chemical Company

Light and Colour

There is no need to put a hand into a glove to know of what it is made. For the eye can often distinguish one material from another by the way the light is reflected from its surface, each different texture producing its own visual effect.

From this subtle interplay of light and surface arises the beauty of the many new materials now appearing in a multitude of shades—thanks to the use of dyes.

ICI dyes. Ad. John R. Barker. c. 1946.
Imperial Chemical Industries Ltd

Kia-Ora, orange drink. Ad. F. H. K. Henrion. 1942.
Kia-Ora Ltd

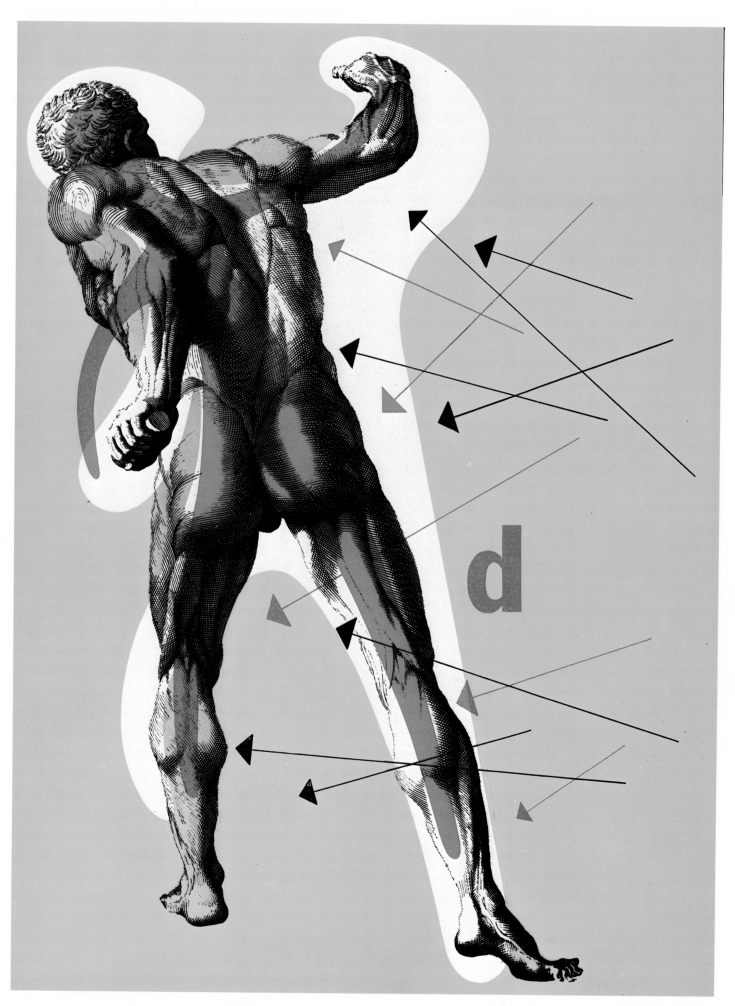

Pharmaceuticals display design. Matthew Leibowitz. 1947. Sharp & Dohme

Caesar and Cleopatra, motion picture. Ad. 1946. United Artists Corp

Joan of Arc, motion picture. Ad. 1948. Sierra Pictures

Coming in 1949

JOAN OF ARC

starring INGRID

BERGMAN

COLOR BY TECHNICOLOR

Adele Simpson's charming dress for daylight dining in a wonderful new **Cotton Taffeta** from the

Wesley Simpson Custom Fabrics collection. This exciting new fabric Spoven by Ponemah has a soft iridescent

bloom and a crisp silky texture—is unbelievably lovely in rich dark colors.

WESLEY SIMPSON

Scarfs, Dress and Decorative Fabrics 215 West 40th St., New York 18, N.Y.

Wesley Simpson, custom fabrics. Ad. John Rawlings. 1949. Wesley Simpson

"*Beauty is rather a light that plays over the symmetry of things than that symmetry itself*" — PLOTINUS

Nylons so unbelievably sheer, so clear they seem a shadow of beauty itself. Yet, they've endurance, too, these 15 denier Bryan beauties...in 54 or 66 gauge. New: dark-hued "Soubrette" with a dashing *black* heel, foot...54 gauge.

BEAUTIFUL
Bryans
THE BREATHTAKING NYLONS

Bryan nylons. Ad. Salvador Dali. 1948. Bryan Fall Fashion Mills Inc

MEN OF
DISTINCTION

Men of distinction and, indeed, all
motorists who appreciate smooth,
sure straight line braking action—
prefer Lockheed Hydraulic Brakes.

LOCKHEED
(REGD. TRADE MARK)
hydraulic brakes

THE SAFEST BRAKES IN THE WORLD

AUTOMOTIVE PRODUCTS COMPANY LTD · LEAMINGTON SPA

C.J.L.

*"I don't know what we'll do with it in a New York
apartment—but he just couldn't resist the U·S·S label!"*

This label is your guide

to quality steel when you buy:

SHOVELS   BED SPRINGS   TOOLS   WHEELBARROWS   BATH TUBS

UNITED STATES STEEL

UNITED STATES STEEL CORPORATION OF DELAWARE, 436 SEVENTH AVENUE, PITTSBURGH 30, PA.
AMERICAN BRIDGE COMPANY • AMERICAN STEEL & WIRE COMPANY and CYCLONE FENCE DIVISION
CARNEGIE-ILLINOIS STEEL CORPORATION • COLUMBIA STEEL COMPANY • CONSOLIDATED WESTERN STEEL CORPORATION
GERRARD STEEL STRAPPING COMPANY • NATIONAL TUBE COMPANY • OIL WELL SUPPLY COMPANY • UNION SUPPLY COMPANY
TENNESSEE COAL, IRON & RAILROAD COMPANY • VIRGINIA BRIDGE COMPANY • UNITED STATES STEEL EXPORT COMPANY
UNITED STATES STEEL PRODUCTS COMPANY • UNITED STATES STEEL SUPPLY COMPANY • UNIVERSAL ATLAS CEMENT COMPANY

Lockheed hydraulic brakes. Ad. Raymond Tooby. 1953.
Automotive Products Company Ltd

U.S. Steel. Ad. Gluyas Williams. 1950.
United States Steel Corporation of Delaware

OPPOSITE
Shell X-100 Motor Oil. Ad. Boris Artzybasheff. 1951.
Shell Oil Company

Your engine makes this much *acid* every day

...And it's Acid Action - not friction that causes 90% of engine wear!

NEW *alkaline* Shell X-100 Motor Oil
neutralizes Acid Action

It's not *friction* but *acid action* that causes 90% of engine wear! To neutralize the harmful effect of the pint or more of acid formed in average daily driving, Shell Research has produced an *alkaline* motor oil— Shell X-100. Fortified with alkaline "X" safety factors, it neutralizes the acid action, prolonging the life of your engine.

The new Shell X-100 is a Premium Motor Oil. It is a Heavy Duty Motor Oil. In addition, it possesses cleansing factors which help prevent deposits that would foul your engine.

Shell X-100 is the finest motor oil money can buy. Let your Shell dealer give your engine the protection of this new alkaline Shell X-100 Motor Oil today.

It's Incomparable!

Lucky Strike cigarettes. Ad (Marlene Dietrich). © 1950.
The American Tobacco Company

Camel cigarettes. Ad (John Wayne). 1954.
R. J. Reynolds Tobacco Company

Philip Morris cigarettes. Ad (Lucille Ball). 1953.
Philip Morris & Co. Ltd, Inc

Chesterfield cigarettes. Ad (Ronald Reagan). 1950. Liggett & Myers Tobacco Co

I've found me a wonderful WAVE!

MARY MARTIN
of Broadway's all-time smash hit
"South Pacific"
Vital part of every costume
she wears: her
RAYVE HOME PERMANENT

"Six nights every week and twice on Wednesdays and Saturdays—my hair gets this sudsing," says Mary Martin, "and all it gets afterward to make it presentable is a few quick licks with a brush. That's why Rayve Home Permanent is so wonderful—it really does make my hair behave as if it were naturally curly."

Energetic as the rest of her, Mary Martin's curls grow so fast that in order to be short enough for that on-stage shampoo, they must be cut weekly, permanented every three weeks.

"Yes, I have to put up 72 curls every 3 weeks! Good thing for me that Rayve's so easy on your hair!"

"You wouldn't think I'd have any hair left, would you?" she inquires in that warm, confiding voice of hers. "But the truth is, my darn hair has never been healthier! Rayve is very, very easy on your hair. I've tried them all, believe me—and really and truly there's a difference between a Rayve Permanent and the rest. You really do get a softer, more natural curl.

"Your hair actually has a *sheen* afterwards—honest! Almost as if you'd been using a hair conditioner, instead of putting in a permanent. I don't know too much about chemistry, but I understand Rayve waving lotion is unique—a different creaming agent, a different wetting agent, and so forth. Anyhow, I know the *results* are unique. You really do get a shinier, softer, more natural curl . . . you really do!

"Well! As you might gather, I'm delighted with it *You* see what *you* think of it!"

The delighted audience all but dances in the aisles nightly as Mary Martin sings "I'm Gonna Wash That Man Right Out of My Hair"—and shampoos her celebrated **crop** with *real* suds. All this inspired "business" was her own idea.

Rayve, home wave and shampoo. Ad (Mary Martin). 1950. Lever Bros. Company

From experience comes faith...

When you are very young you offer hand and heart to any living thing. Everyone is your friend.

Then come lessons in judgment. Mother's gentle warnings, experience earned wherever your life may lead, teach you many things: to listen for the hard facts behind soft words; to look for the evidence of integrity. Experience replaces simple trust with judgment in where to place your faith.

Blood plasma, sulfa drugs, penicillin and many other medicinals produced by E. R. Squibb & Sons mean life itself. Few services to man call for greater experience and trust than the services of the pharmaceutical manufacturer.

The priceless ingredient of every product is the honor and integrity of its maker.

SQUIBB
© E. R. S & S

Squibb, pharmaceutical products. Ad. Reeve Limebruner. c. 1951. E. R. Squibb & Sons

Texaco Fire-Chief Gasoline. Ad. Keith Ward. 1954.
The Texas Company

It's Father's Day in the FOUR ROSES SOCIETY

Four Roses whiskey. Ad. Howard Zieff. 1959.
Four Roses Distillers Company

'Black & White' Scotch Whiskey. Ad. 1954.
James Buchanan & Co., Ltd

"and a man's next best friend is his Arrow Shirt!"

Cluett, Peabody & Co., Inc..

Arrow Shirts. Ad. Ylla/Jack Anthony. 1952. Cluett, Peabody & Co., Inc

How to retire...and keep your head above water

MONY can <u>guarantee</u> a retirement income for <u>you</u>

If you're like most of us, there's only one way you can *guarantee* a retirement income you cannot outlive...no matter how *long* you live. That guarantee is with life insurance. And here's why we suggest MONY.

Today, MONY offers you life insurance at a *discount*—lower rates on larger poli-

cies. That means MONY can make it easier for you to own more life insurance *at a lower cost than you'd expect*. This larger MONY policy can also mean extra income to make your retirement years more comfortable.

Learn more by sending for MONY's free booklet, "Your Future Is In Your Hands."

MUTUAL **O F N E W** Y**ORK**
The Mutual Life Insurance Company Of New York, New York, N.Y.
Sales and service offices located throughout the United States and in Canada

For Life, Accident & Sickness, Group Insurance, Pension Plans, **MONY** TODAY MEANS **MONEY** TOMORROW!

FREE BOOKLET
TELLS WAYS TO PLAN
YOUR RETIREMENT

MONY, Dept. L-79
B'way at 55th Street
New York 19, N. Y.

I would like a copy of MONY's free booklet, "Your Future Is In Your Hands."

Name_____
Address_____
City_____Zone_____
County_____State_____
Occupation_____
Date of Birth_____

MONY, life insurance. Ad. Frank Cowan. 1959.
The Mutual Life Insurance Company of New York

TALENT SCOUT. Mathes art directors keep scanning the horizon for new approaches. They are always on the lookout for work with a flair. It is this fresh viewpoint which makes the difference between advertising that stands still and advertising that stands out...*and sells.*
J.M.MATHES,INC..Advertising
260 Madison Avenue, New York 16, N. Y.

J. M. Mathes, advertising agency. Ad. Carter Jones.
1954. J. M. Mathes, Inc

*at
C.P.V.
the
marketing
and
creative men
see eye to eye*

CPV, advertising and marketing. Ad. 1959.
Colman, Prentis & Varley Ltd

COLMAN PRENTIS & VARLEY LTD
ADVERTISING AND MARKETING
*AFFILIATE OFFICES IN BOGOTA BRUSSELS
CARACAS MILAN PARIS PORT-OF-SPAIN
SINGAPORE TORONTO
AND 64 OVERSEAS ASSOCIATES*

How to avoid dry, unruly "orang-utan hair"

New greaseless way to keep your hair neat all day

New Vitalis with V-7 prevents dryness, makes hair easy to manage

If you dislike over-oily hair tonics, here's good news. New Vitalis keeps hair in place with V-7, the *greaseless* grooming discovery.

You can use Vitalis as often as you like—even every day—yet never have an over-slick, plastered-down look.

What's more, it gives you wonderful protection from dry hair and scalp. And tests show it kills on contact germs many doctors associate with infectious dandruff—as no mere cream or oil dressing can.

Try new Vitalis with V-7. You'll *like* it.

New VITALIS® Hair Tonic with V-7.®

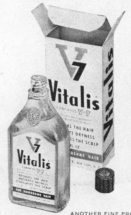

NEW VITALIS   **MESSY OILS**

"TISSUE TEST" proves greaseless Vitalis outdates messy oils

In an independent testing laboratory, Vitalis and leading cream and oil tonics were applied in the normal way. Hair was combed and then wiped with cleansing tissue. Unretouched photographs above show the difference in results!

ANOTHER FINE PRODUCT OF BRISTOL-MYERS

New Vitalis Hair Tonic. Ad. 1955. Bristol-Myers Co

ENKA RAYON

THE SOFT ELEGANCE OF CREPE

*A Larry Aldrich completely tucked dress
in Hess Goldsmith's Velura—
woven with Enka Rayon and acetate.
Bonwit Teller, New York
Joseph Horne, Pittsburgh
I. Magnin, California-Seattle
Montaldo Shops*

AMERICAN ENKA CORPORATION
206 MADISON AVE., NEW YORK 16, N.Y.

SOFA BY DUNBAR

SCAVULLO

HAT BY JOHN FREDERICS

Enka Rayon. Ad. Francesco Scavullo. 1952. American Enka Corporation

American Fabrics magazine. Cover. Saul Steinberg. 1950. Reporter Publications, Inc

american fabrics

STEINBERG

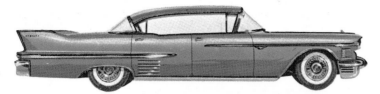

The magnificent Cadillac car has long been the great personal favorite of the American lady. But seldom in our memory has a Cadillac so thoroughly captivated her as has the "car of cars" for 1958. Certainly, the reasons for this are legion. There are its new beauty and elegance, its new Fleetwood luxury, its new ease of driving and handling, its extraordinary quiet and smoothness of ride, and its many new passenger conveniences. We cordially invite you to visit your dealer's showroom soon to investigate all of these Cadillac virtues for yourself. You will be his welcome guest at any time.

CADILLAC MOTOR CAR DIVISION • GENERAL MOTORS CORPORATION

Safety Plate Glass Used Exclusively In All Models

Gown by Scaasi

Cadillac. Ad. Horst P. Horst. 1958. General Motors Corporation

De Beers diamonds. Ad. Raoul Dufy. 1951. De Beers Consolidated Mines Ltd

Seaside Romance . . . painted for the De Beers Collection by Raoul Dufy

The prices shown were secured for your guidance through a nationwide check in July, 1951. Jewelers were asked for the prices of their top-grade engagement ring diamonds (unmounted) in the weights indicated. The result is a range of prices, varying according to the qualities offered by different jewelers. Exceptionally fine diamonds are higher priced (Exact weights shown are infrequent.) Add Federal tax.

WHEN CHOOSING YOUR ENGAGEMENT STONE . . . remember color, cutting, and clarity, as well as carat weight, contribute to a diamond's beauty and value. It is important to seek the counsel of a trusted jeweler. He will help you find the size and quality and style of stone that is in keeping with your preferences, and what you wish to spend.

A DIAMOND IS FOREVER

¼ carat (25 points) $90 to $185
½ carat (50 points) $220 to $450
1 carat (100 points) $625 to $1105
2 carats (200 points) $1600 to $2835

N. W. AYER & SON

Keeper of dreams   No flower ever was so gay, no sun so bright, as your engagement diamond. Token of love, guardian of dreams, it will lend its lovely light to all your years. Guiding your thoughts to one another through days of parting, it will dance for joy at your reunions. And all the happy moments, all the changes and responsibilities you share, will be recorded in its magic depths. Though it be modest in cost, choose your diamond with care, for nothing else on earth can take its place. And...may your happiness last as long as your diamond.

De Beers Consolidated Mines, Ltd.

fiber of the ages ... fashion of the moment

Silk

Timeless, ever opportune ... silk is fashion's most urgent inspiration
and most serene expression ... your own love of beauty translated into fabric.

International SILK Association (U.S.A.) Inc. 489 Fifth Avenue, New York 17, N.Y.

International Silk Congress, London. Ad.
Cecil Beaton. 1951.
Silk & Rayon Users Association

TOP RIGHT:
Advertisement for silk. Leslie Gill. c. 1954.
International Silk Association (U.S.A.) Inc

RIGHT:
'Shellguide'. Booklet illustration. Edith Hilder.
1954. Shell-Mex Ltd

Modess . . . because. Ad. Cecil Beaton. 1951. Personal Products Corp

Engineering to the Nth power....

O'er the ramparts we watch as we track a guided missile aimed at an attacking enemy or his home base. Yes, missiles may fight tomorrow's battles or prevent them. And Convair, the *only* company developing and building *every* basic type of aircraft, has a guided missile team helping America achieve a weapons system for *every* conceivable mission. Watch for new ramparts of peace, built through engineering that aims at the maximum of power . . . *the Nth Power!* **CONVAIR**

SAN DIEGO & POMONA, CALIFORNIA · FORT WORTH & DAINGERFIELD, TEXAS

Convair aircraft. Ad. R. Wicks/M. Henninger. 1952. General Dynamics Corp

Boeing 707 and 720 jetliners. Ad. 1958. Boeing Airplane Co.

Soon leading airlines, flying Boeing jetliners, will cut your travel time in half!

Within a few months now, you can enjoy travel so excitingly different it will give new meaning to time and distance. In Boeing 707s, flown by leading airlines, you'll cross continents and seas in half the time required by conventional aircraft. The U. S. will be only four and a half hours wide; the Atlantic, six. You *could* make a round trip to Europe in a day! Whatever your destination, you'll arrive rested and refreshed, for travel aboard a Boeing jetliner is incredibly smooth, quiet, and completely free of fatiguing vibration. You'll relax in a cabin more spacious, more luxuriously appointed than any now aloft. In addition, you'll cruise through calm upper skies, far above the weather. Aboard the superb Boeing 707 —or its shorter-range sister ship, the 720—you'll be flying in the most thoroughly flight-tested aircraft ever to enter commercial service.

BOEING 707 and 720

Advertisement for silk. Eugene Berman.
1951. International Silk Association

Nice. Poster. Henri Matisse. 1948.
French National Tourist Office

Intoxication perfume. Ad (detail). Richard
Lindner. 1953. D'Orsay Sales Co

Agreed! No bourbon anywhere is more deluxe
than Walker's DeLuxe

Straight bourbon, of course—7 years smooth—elegant in taste

STRAIGHT BOURBON WHISKEY • 7 YEARS OLD • 86 PROOF • HIRAM WALKER & SONS INC., PEORIA, ILL.

Walker's DeLuxe bourbon. Ad. Ludwig Bemelmans. c. 1952. Hiram Walker & Sons Inc

Marilyn Monroe. Publicity photo, *Gentlemen Prefer Blondes*, motion picture. 1953. 20th Century-Fox Film Corporation

TOP LEFT:
Fly to U.S.A. by B.O.A.C. Poster. Phoenix Studios. c. 1954. British Overseas Airways Corporation

LEFT:
Air Express. Ad (detail). Ralph Steiner. 1953. Air Express International Corp

Du magazine. Cover (New Orleans). Emil Schulthess. 1955. Conzett & Huber, Zurich

Lemon Hart rum. Poster. Ronald Searle. 1956.
United Rum Merchants

Eno's 'Fruit Salt'. Poster. Tom Eckersley. 1952.
J. C. Eno Ltd

Grand Marnier, orange liqueur. Ad. Chester Gore Company.
c. 1959. Carillon Importers Ltd

Coronet brandy. Ad. Paul Rand. 1951. Coronet V.S.Q. Brandy Dist. Corp

Kayser: Hosiery, Gloves, Lingerie. Ad (detail).
Saul Bolasni. 1951. Kayser-Roth Corp

Bear Brand stockings. Ad. 1950. Howard Ford Co., Ltd

Van Raalte gloves. Ad. 1951. Van Raalte Co., Inc

RITA HAYWORTH
STARRING IN
"AFFAIR IN TRINIDAD"
A COLUMBIA PICTURES
CORPORATION RELEASE
DRESS BY JEAN LOUIS.

Rita Hayworth
danced 36 miles
in these wispy
MOJUD *"MAGIC·MOTION"*
stockings

**In one of the most
sensational dances ever screened...
ravishing Rita gave her Mojuds
more wear than *you* might in a year!**

36 miles of dancing! In one of the most sinuous dance routines in history! What a gruelling test this glamorous star gave to a pair of wispy Mojud stockings.

Rita Hayworth swirled, twirled, whirled in them. For three weeks of rehearsal! For 36 hours before the camera!

The whole WORLD'S eyes (as well as the camera's) are on this woman who has been called "The Love Goddess of America". Her stockings MUST fit and flatter. That's why Rita Hayworth wears Mojud ...the stockings with Magic-Motion...extra "give" and spring-back in the knit.

Just think of what Mojuds will do for *you!*

stockings by
MOJUD®

Remember, there's lovely Lingerie by Mojud, too. At fine stores everywhere. For nearest dealer write Mojud Hosiery Co., Inc., 385 Fifth Ave., New York 16, N. Y. ©1952

Mojud 'Magic-Motion' stockings. Ad. 1952. Mojud Hosiery Co., Inc

BIG GAME. Hunt up a pencil and join these dots with lines. Huzzah! You'll see Tony, the famous Sugar Frosted Flakes tiger, showing how ferociously fond he is of a new kind of breakfast that's fun to eat.

Tony the Tiger says: **"Gr-r-reat!"**

Smart folks will finish this picture with a spoon. Their starting point is the flavor of these bigger, crisper flakes of corn that sparkle all over with Kellogg's secret sugar frosting. Gr-r-reat!

Kellogg's **SUGAR FROSTED FLAKES**

Kellogg's SUGAR FROSTED FLAKES

Kellogg's Sugar Frosted Flakes. Ad.
Jack Kapeo/E. Van Baerle. 1954. The Kellogg Company

Who ate my Post Toasties?

Here's a young lady who brooks
no interference with her lawful rights.
When it comes to corn flakes, it's gotta be
Post Toasties and nothing else but—they're so crisp,
so golden-tasting, so sweet and special. So hurry to the store,
Mother, and tell the man you want some more—right now!
For goodness sake—get Post Toasties!

Post Toasties, breakfast food. Ad.
Whitney Darrow, Jr. 1959. General Foods Corp

Simoniz vinyl floor wax. Ad (detail).
Whitney Darrow, Jr. 1959. The Simoniz Co

Jell-O dessert. Ad. Jack Welch. © 1954. General Foods Corp

When I'm making Jell-O
I wish I were a turtle

...because then I could
show folks how quick Jell-O
is to fix. (You can be as
slow as a turtle and <u>still</u>
turn out magnificent desserts
in no time!)*

Now's the time for **JELL-O**
BRAND
GELATIN DESSERT
SIX DELICIOUS FLAVORS

*Jell-O now sets in *30* minutes, the new Quick-Set Way.
Directions on the package.

Jell-O is a registered trade-mark of General Foods Corporation

Copyright 1954, General Foods Corp.

IT'S FUN TO 'PHONE!

Turn a few minutes into fun by calling a friend or loved one. Whether it's
down the street, or across the country, a sunny get-together makes the day
a lot brighter. Lonely feelings are laughed away by a cheerful visit by telephone.
So treat yourself to a welcome break and just for fun—call someone!

BELL TELEPHONE SYSTEM

Bell Telephone System: 'Betsy Bell'. Ad. Peter Hawley. 1958. American Telephone & Telegraph Co

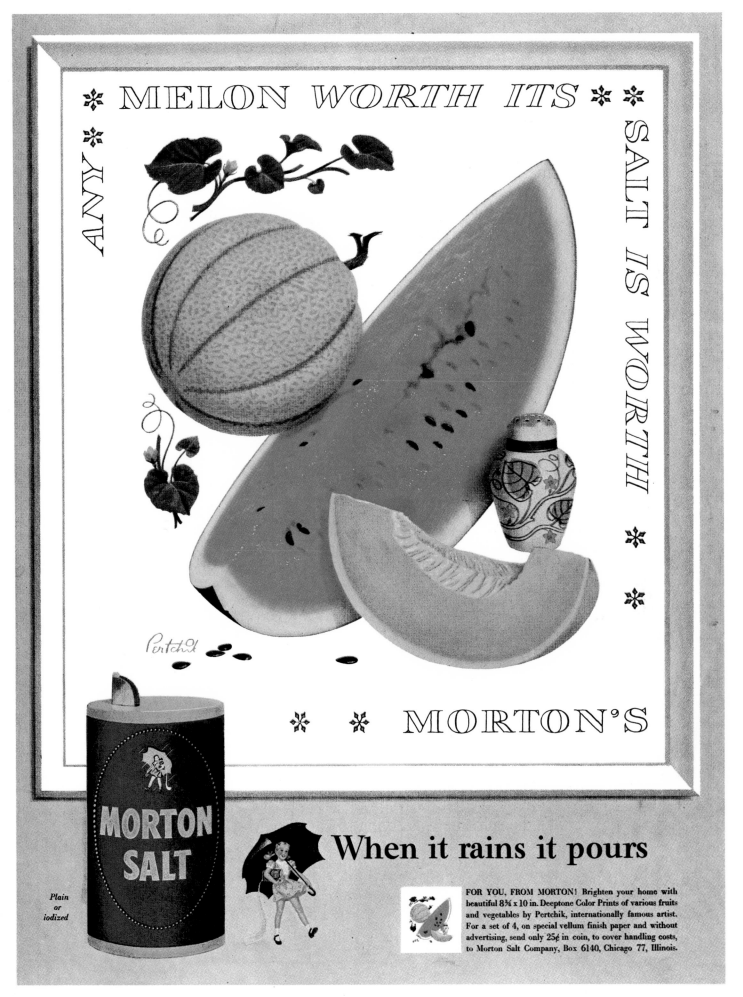

Morton Salt. Ad. Harriet Pertchik.1954. Morton Salt Company

Huntley & Palmer's Biscuits. Ad. Pauline Baynes. 1952.
Huntley & Palmer Ltd

Mackintosh's 'Quality Street', toffees and chocolates. Ad.
1954. John Mackintosh & Sons Inc

LEFT:
Standard and Triumph cars. Ad. 1954.
The Standard Motor Co., Ltd

OPPOSITE:
Westinghouse, light bulbs. Ad. 1951.
Westinghouse Electric Corp

"WE LIGHT OUR HOUSE WITH
WESTINGHOUSE . . . THE
BRIGHTEST BUY
IN BULBS"

YOU CAN BE SURE...IF IT'S
Westinghouse

Neither sun nor sea nor salt air can di

This is the year you could buy
suit to see you through the su
of course, you like to change yo
for the fun of it. And the chance
be able to resist doing just that.
For this is the year you'll w
made with Chromspun, the Eastm

◄ **PHOTOGRAPHED UNDER WATER** through viewing
windows of the pool at Marlin Beach Hotel, Fort
Lauderdale, Florida. Chlorinated yes, but the swim
suit color keeps because it's color-locked Chromspun.

LEFT:
Catalina, swim suits. Ad (detail). © 1954. Catalina, Inc

ABOVE:
Eastman Chromspun acetate fiber. Ad (detail). 1954.
Eastman Chemical Products, Inc

OPPOSITE:
Nothing *Satisfies* like coffee. Ad (detail). © 1951.
Pan-American Coffee Bureau

OPPOSITE RIGHT:
Jantzen, swim suits. Ad. Peter Hawley. 1951.
Jantzen Knitting Mills, Inc

-in color of swim suits made with Chromspun

wing color locked in tight.
Against the sea. Against such
ng hazards as salt air, atmos-
piration, or crocking all over
ch bag.

lors have inspired a whole
suit fashions: pretty pastels,

bold, bright, new color combinations and dra-
matic contrasts of darks with white. You're
going to love the way they look against your tan.

And you're also going to love the way swim suits
made with Chromspun feel against your skin,
their luxurious texture, the quick way they dry.
There couldn't be a more decorative combina-

tion, all summer long, than you and Chromspun
in the swim. You'll find Chromspun swim suits
and other good things made of color-locked
Chromspun, to wear and to decorate your home,
at your favorite department store now.

*All Chromspun colors have passed Class L6,
AATCC tests for light fastness.*

CHROMSPUN is the color-locked EASTMAN acetate fiber

EASTMAN CHEMICAL PRODUCTS, INC., SUBSIDIARY OF EASTMAN KODAK COMPANY, 260-MADISON AVENUE, NEW YORK 16, N. Y.

for romancin'...

and entrancin'

...there's nothing like a Jantzen!

for that matter there's nothing like a Jantzen for swimming
and slimming...nothing like the way a Jantzen fits, feels and
looks...nothing like the wonderful figure-making job a Jantzen
does...nothing like the marvelous Jantzen swim suit fabrics...
in particular, Jantzen Nylastic, the magic-moulding fast-drying
special Jantzen blend of nylon and laton, the finest swim
suit fabric ever made. Girl's suit, detailed for romance, with
marvelous Jantzen mouldable Stay-Bra 15.95...man's speed-cut
racers 5.95...terrific colors for everybody...at most stores.

Jantzen
Nylastic
nylon-with-laton
swim suits

Matching Jantzen swim caps
and Jandals in stunning pastels

JANTZEN, PORTLAND 14, OREGON

"What a lifesaver...
Joe's making Coffee!"

'M-m-m! Nothing *Smells* as Good as Coffee!'
Somehow, the fragrance of coffee is even
more appealing than usual after a long cool
swim. It's one of the richest, most tempting
aromas in the world. Sort of sets you up
just thinking about it!

'M-m-m! Nothing *Tastes* as Good as Coffee!'
Joe's rich, full-strength coffee would glad-
den the heart of anybody. Iced or hot—
at home, by the shore or in your favorite
restaurant—no other beverage gives so much
for so little.

HOT or ICED

"*Nothing Satisfies Like Coffee!*"

A New Yorker, a bit of a mystic,
Found his guide a shade unrealistic
For the Windsor she knew
Was no longer on view
The guides on London Transport conducted coach tours are up to date and
fresh and blood too. Green line routes 704, 706, 718 and 725 also go to Windsor.

London Transport, conducted coach tours. Poster.
John Bainbridge. 1957. London Transport Executive

A highwayman found street congestion
Made robbery out of the question
With life one long hold up
His assets were sold up

And he was driven underground* to the fresh air and quiet
of Epping Forest - a fool's paradise, as his horse remarked!

*Central Line, of course, to Loughton or Theydon Bois

Underground Railway. Poster. John Bainbridge. 1957.
London Transport Executive

AMERICAN AIRLINES

TO

ENGLAND

OPPOSITE:
Holiday magazine. Cover. George Giusti. 1958.
Curtis Publishing Company

Travel poster. E. McKnight Kauffer. 1951.
American Airlines Inc

HOLIDAY

APRIL 1958 · 50¢

ENGLAND

Giusti

Over the hills and far away . . .

See the immaculate lines and well mannered obedience of the Riley
and you might think it was a town car. But you will find it never
so happy as when the hedgerows are flying past in the seventies
or when a rolling road gives scope to its superb steering and
incomparable road-holding.

There's a famous racing lineage behind the Riley and you need an
open road to appreciate it to the full.

2½ litre Saloon. 1½ litre Saloon.

Riley - as old as the industry - as modern as the hour

RILEY MOTORS LIMITED, *Sales Division*, **COWLEY, OXFORD**
London Showrooms: RILEY CARS, 55-56 PALL MALL, S.W.1   Overseas Business: Nuffield Exports Ltd, Oxford and 41 Piccadilly, London, W.1

Riley. Ad. Chris O. Watkins. 1952. Riley Motors Limited

Setting the Style

From well-groomed head to well-shod feet she's elegance
itself. The same pride—and care—is reflected in her car. Immaculate
interior . . . brilliant bodywork . . . gleaming glass and chromium . . . and,
to set off the whole, the smartness of Dunlop White Sidewall tyres.
Distinctive, dependable and safe, these tyres—in 'Dunlop',
Dunlop Fort and Roadspeed types—will enhance the design and
colour of *your* car. Whether or not you
choose White Sidewall, do make sure
you keep to Dunlop—with or without
the tube, as you please.

DUNLOP

makes the tyre y*ou* want

Dunlop tyres. Ad. Michie. 1956. Dunlop Rubber Co., Ltd

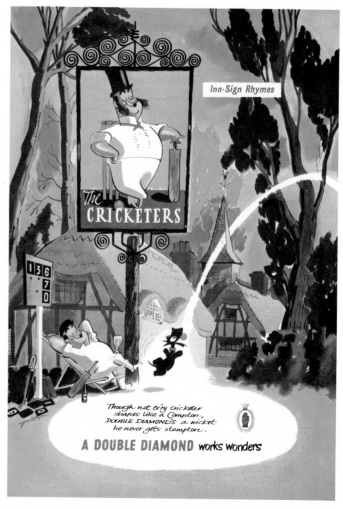

Inn-Sign Rhymes

The CRICKETERS

*Though not ev'ry cricketer
shapes like a Compton,
DOUBLE DIAMOND'S a wicket
he never gets stompton.*

A DOUBLE DIAMOND works wonders

Double Diamond beer. Ad. Peter Probyn. 1956.
Ind Coope & Allsop Ltd

232

IT'S WATCH INSPECTION TIME, SEPTEMBER 9-18.

WHAT MAKES IT TICK?

WHEN you listen to your watch, it speaks not only of the passing of the seconds but of the skills of all the men whose efforts have gone into its perfection.

To a watchmaker, your watch is like a living thing. His world is as tiny as the watch he is working on—and as large as the history of recorded time.

Your watch ticks 432,000 times a day—as the lever jewels strike the escape wheel. The constancy of this heartbeat determines the accuracy of your watch, the big difference between a fine Swiss jeweled-lever watch and an ordinary watch. For a fine Swiss watch is painstakingly precisioned —from the balance wheel that travels 3600 miles a year to the tiniest screw, no bigger than this period → .

Whether you're buying a new watch, or having a watch serviced, your jeweler will show you what Swiss craftsmanship means to you in beauty, accuracy, value—and in the ease and economy of servicing. No wonder 7 out of 10 jewelers wear fine Swiss watches themselves! *For the gifts you'll give with pride, let your jeweler be your guide.*

The Watchmakers of Switzerland

Time is the Art of the Swiss

© 1954 Swiss Federation of Watch Manufacturers

What makes it tick? Ad. Norman Rockwell. © 1954. Swiss Federation of Watchmakers

Liberty department store. Poster. Ashley Havinden.
1951. Liberty & Co., Limited, London

Number Seven—by Abdulla. Ad. P. Monnerat. 1955.
Abdulla & Company Limited

Good books . . . Poster. George Krikorian. 1951.
The New York Times

Travel booklet. Cover. Raymond Peynet. 1955.
Air France

TOP LEFT:
Schweppes, table waters. Ad. George Him. 1956.
Schweppes Co., Ltd

LEFT:
Gothic Art, Spain. Poster. Orteys. 1959.
Dirección General de Turismo

Harvey-Woods' 'Stop Red' lingerie. Ad.
Jean Miller/Allen Sneath. 1958. York Knitting Mills Ltd

Alfred Hitchcock's *Vertigo,* motion picture. Ad.
Saul Bass. © 1958. Paramount Pictures Corporation

Ascot, cigarette lighter. Ad. Bob Wall. 1952.
American Safety Razor Corp

"Sans Hésiter" lipstick. Ad. René Gruau. 1950. Paul Baudecroux

Duco® Enamel
Semi-Gloss
Jonquil Yellow

Duco Enamel
Spray Magic
Primrose Yellow

Flow Kote®
Wall Paint
Periwinkle Blue

Custom Color
Semi-Gloss
No. 1318

Look under "Paint" in the Classified Telephone Directory for your nearest Du Pont Paint Dealer

If you're painting something new, or renewing something old . . .

the beauty _lasts_ when you paint with the finest . . . DUPONT paints

REG U S PAT OFF

Better Things for Better Living . . . through Chemistry

Dupont paints. Ad. 1958. E. I. Dupont de Nemours & Co

Fiberglas-reinforced plastics. Ad. 1958. Owens-Corning Fiberglas Corporation

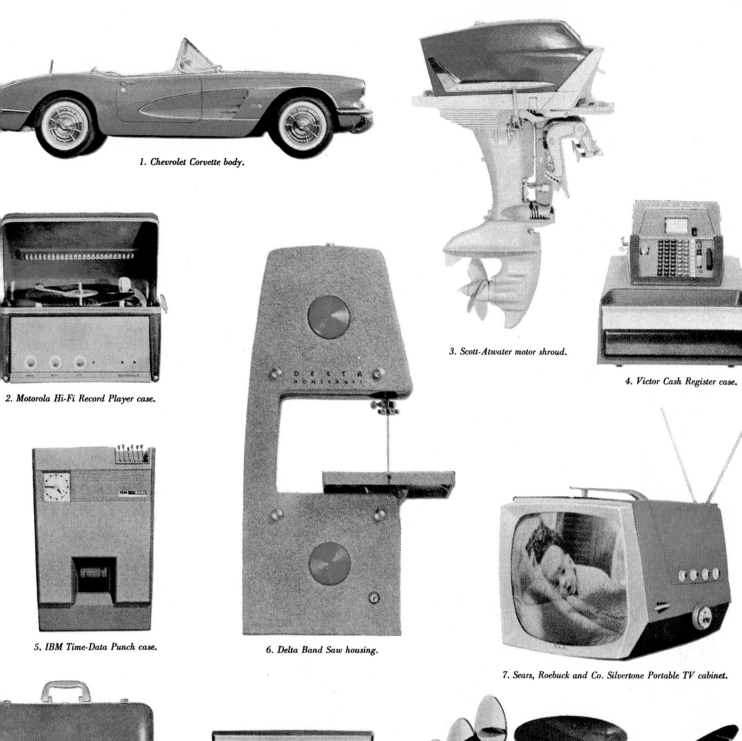

1. Chevrolet Corvette body.

2. Motorola Hi-Fi Record Player case.

3. Scott-Atwater motor shroud.

4. Victor Cash Register case.

5. IBM Time-Data Punch case.

6. Delta Band Saw housing.

7. Sears, Roebuck and Co. Silvertone Portable TV cabinet.

8. Koch Luggage.

9. Town and Country mail box.

10. Lockheed WV-2E radome housing.

Why products turn out better when the makers turn to Fiberglas*

e's no end to the wonderful colors, graceful shapes, permanent finishes that Fiberglas-reinforced plas- bring to a wider and wider variety of products. ob or small, home or industry, these versatile new ics are molding permanent color, quality and rmance into the smartest looking products today.

They have the strength and durability to take it. Whatever the weather or temperature, they won't fade, warp, rust or rot. When long, hard wear is expected, they won't chip, crack or peel. The fact is, products made with Fiberglas-reinforced plastics have built-in beauty and need little or no upkeep.

MANUFACTURERS: Add new beauty and utility to the products you make. Produce them faster, easier at lower cost, with Fiberglas-reinforced plastics! To find out how, write: Owens-Corning Fiberglas Corporation, Dept. 10G-7, 598 Madison Ave., New York 22, N. Y.

OWENS-CORNING
FIBERGLAS

*T-M. (Reg. U.S. Pat. Off.) O-C.F. Corp.

f above products: 1. Molded Fiber Glass Body Co., Ashtabula, Ohio. ● 2. Minnesota Mining & Mfg. Co., St. Paul, Minn. ● 3. G. B. Lewis Co., Watertown, Wis. and General Tire & Rubber Co., Marion, Ind. ● 4. Camfield Fiberglas Plastics, Inc., Zeeland, Mich. ● 5, 6. Molded s Co., Ashtabula, Ohio. ● 7. General American Transportation Corp., Chicago, Ill. ● 8. H. Koch and Sons, Corte Madera, Cal. ● 9. Plastic Products Corp., Bedford Heights, Ohio. ● 10. Zenith Plastics Co., Subsidiary of Minnesota Mining & Mfg. Co., Gardena, Calif.

The Trigère Cult

087506
IOBE TICKET COMPANY, HILA
ADMIT ONE
087506
FIFTH NEW YORK
Film Festival·Lincoln Center
PHILHARMONIC HALL SEPTEMBER 20-30

1960-1980

In 1960, as Eisenhower's second term was ending, John F. Kennedy, age forty-three, defeated Richard M. Nixon at the polls to become the first Catholic President of the United States, and the youngest since Theodore Roosevelt.

In England, five years earlier, Prime Minister Churchill, age eighty, retired in favour of Anthony Eden. In 1956 squabbles with President Nasser over oil and the Suez Canal flared up, and England, joined by France, attacked Egypt. This on top of Israel's simultaneous move against her Arab neighbour, aroused such worldwide disapproval that a dispirited Eden resigned, to be succeeded by Harold Macmillan who, in turn, was succeeded in 1963 by Sir Alec Douglas-Home.

Even though the free world and the Soviet dictatorships were at such loggerheads that in 1960 Nikita Khrushchev snatched off a shoe and pounded the speaker's rostrum at the United Nations as hard as he could with it—there was still hope that tempers wouldn't bring the cold war to a boil. Things were already so red—and hot—in Fidel Castro's communist Cuba that Eisenhower severed diplomatic ties with the dictatorship on January 3, 1961.

There were also fears that efforts to block communism in Vietnam might involve the United States as deeply as Korea had in 1950, when three years of undeclared war ended in a stalemate.

Meanwhile the space race intensified. After sending up two dogs—with rats, mice, and fleas as fellow travellers—the Soviets, on April 12, 1961, sent 'cosmonaut' Yuri Gagarin spinning round the earth in Sputnik. Three weeks later it was Cape Canaveral's turn to lift 'astronaut' Alan B. Shepard, Jr., 115 miles into space. The following February up went the first American, John H. Glenn, Jr., to orbit the earth three times.

Kennedy (page 244) promised that before the decade was out man would reach the moon, and on July 21, 1969, three men succeeded (page 278). Hundreds of millions dropped everything to watch TV, hardly believing their eyes as Neil A. Armstrong and Edwin E. Aldrin landed Apollo on the moon and then, moving like slowly bouncing balloons, raised the American flag on the lifeless planet.

In many ways the sixties had started out on a decidedly upbeat note. Never had the English monarchy produced a more handsome or dedicated young couple than the reigning Queen and the Duke of Edinburgh, the Papacy a more humanitarian and popular 'prince' than Pope John XXIII, or the American Presidency a more energetic and glamorous team than the Kennedys. There was a youthful spontaneity and romantic style about everything the Kennedys did, from Jackie's restoration of the Executive Mansion—combining elegance with an authentic sense of history—and the star-spangled manner in which they entertained visiting dignitaries, to such idealistic ventures as the Peace Corps to help poorer nations.

Then came a series of devastating shocks. Peaceful anti-segregation movements met with mob violence, leading in turn to retaliations, burnings, looting, and later, in 1968, to the martyrdom of Martin Luther King, Jr. The East Germans blocked off West Berlin with a gun-manned wall. Russia exploded new bombs in violation of the test-ban treaty and started building missile sites in Cuba. In June 1963 Pope John died, and on November 22 President Kennedy was assassinated in full view of television cameras—a shock that sent off tidal waves of sorrow, dismay, anger throughout the free world. 'America wept . . . not only for its dead young President but for itself,' said *The New York Times*. 'Somehow the worst in the nation had prevailed over the best.'

Meanwhile from Liverpool's Merseyside came a lively up-tempo beat. The Beatles (page 258) with their bushy 'Julius Caesar' hair mops—which Jonathan Miller said reminded him of 'the Midwich cuckoos'—made their first recording in 1962, and by the time they had filmed *A Hard Day's Night* in 1964 and were singing 'I Want to Hold Your Hand' and 'Hold Me Tight', fans by the millions—who would have given their eyeteeth to be given half the chance—greeted them with screams of delight wherever they dared to appear.

While the Beatles became England's most popular export, a rejuvenated England became the most 'in' port of call. Even Paris nodded at Quant's quaint minis—*Le Style Anglais*—and at 'attic Edwardian' for men.

In 1960 Kenneth Tynan had said 'the young are bored. There is the desire to hear breaking glass.' The ensuing *Blow-Up*—typified, in spirit, by Antonioni's film with Vanessa Redgrave, and his *Zabriskie Point*—paralleled the youth rampage of the twenties. But instead of getting merry on gin, it was on wine, or off to wonderland on pot.

As surprise became the soul of fashion, so art moved on from the dip-and-drip excitements of Jackson Pollock to Pop and Op.

David Hockney and Andy Warhol were big news, and among the new gods of the poster—represented on the next pages—were Milton Glaser, Peter Max, David Edward Byrd, and Jacqui Morgan. Not since McKnight Kauffer and Cassandre had graphics been so excitingly different.

Photography was more candid than kind—to the crow's-foot, at least, or sagging chin! The eyes and the undiffused lenses of Alfred Eisenstaedt, Richard Avedon, David Bailey, Irving Penn, and other masters were focused on the truth, out of which developed a pure and powerful imagery ideally suited to advertising. Truth was the watchword of the copywriter, too, since the big clamp-down on false advertising claims. Even cigarettes, it now had to be said, might be harmful to your health.

When the ban was lifted on D. H. Lawrence's *Lady Chatterley's Lover,* novels, plays, and films became increasingly graphic. In 1962 Edward Albee's *Who's Afraid of Virginia Woolf?* described as 'a witches' brew of domestic love/hate', practically blew Broadway audiences out of their seats. But in 1966, when *Who's Afraid* returned as the sizzling vehicle for the world's most famous couple, Richard Burton and Elizabeth Taylor, four-letter words no longer seemed so very different from those of five or six.

On English TV David Frost's lemony and witty *That Was the Week That Was* became in the sixties as rivetingly popular as the romantic *Upstairs, Downstairs* (page 297) was to become—in America too—in the 'recuperative' seventies. Dudley Moore and Jonathan Miller held little sacred in *Beyond the Fringe,* sweetness was hardly the word for *The Rocky Horror Show,* and Anthony Newley's plea was *Stop the World—I Want to Get Off.*

The world that most young people wanted to get off had now been labelled 'The Establishment'. By 1968 the campus revolution was in full swing with 'teach-in' debates on the escalated Vietnam war. Flower children had 'love-ins', and the dedicated hippie, with long locks, bare feet, and periods of quiet meditation, felt closer to nature, to the philosophers and philosophies of the rediscovered East, and to Jesus Christ, who, in 1971, became *Superstar* of the biggest rock musical since *Hair* (pages 270 and 280).

For adventure, nothing in the sixties topped the excitement of super spy James Bond, until all the Agent 007 thrillers—and Sean Connery—were exhausted and author Ian Fleming dead. The swing to science fiction started in 1968 with Stanley Kubrick's dazzlingly ingenious *2001: A Space Odyssey* (page 278). *Star Wars, Star Trek* (page 307), and other strange encounters followed in the seventies.

Lighter film fare found such appealing new entertainers as Peter Sellers, Woody Allen (page 264), Dustin Hoffman, and Barbra Streisand, who recreated Carol Channing's role in the film version of *Hello, Dolly!* (page 274). The first actor to wink at the audience from the screen was Albert Finney in *Tom Jones,* which was such fun that it had to win the 1963 Oscar. The biggest success of the century turned out to be the sweet and wholesome *The Sound of Music,* which in 1965 started grossing more money than any other film in history.

In politics, when President Lyndon B. Johnson decided against running for a second term in 1968, Richard M. Nixon inched ahead of Hubert H. Humphrey, and after re-election in 1972 was just into his second term when up went the curtain on Watergate. Nixon resigned on August 8, 1974, and Gerald Ford did his best to patch things up, but in 1976 the country went out to vote for a new Democrat, Jimmy Carter (page 311).

In 1979 England made history when Conservative Margaret Thatcher defeated Prime Minister James Callaghan, thus becoming famous as the first woman ever to head the British government. That year Israel shook hands with Egypt, and diplomatic smiles were being exchanged between Washington and Peking.

Then, in November 1979, Iran tossed a very hot potato into Carter's lap. After the ailing Shah, who had escaped the revolutionaries, flew from his refuge in Mexico to the United States to be examined in a New York hospital, Muslim students in Teheran seized Americans in the U.S. Embassy and held them hostage against the return of the former ruler. The saga continued with Carter ordering an unfortunate rescue attempt, the Shah being given asylum by the gracious Anwar al-Sadat in Egypt, where he was to die in July 1980, and Carter making an unsuccessful bid for re-election in November. The drama ended with the remaining fifty-two hostages flown to freedom, on the very day Carter was to watch Ronald Reagan (page 199) take over his duties as the fortieth President of the United States of America.

FROM LEFT TO RIGHT:

John F. Kennedy, Election poster. 1960
Pauline Trigère fashion ad by Melvin Sokolsky. 1967
Poster for the Fifth New York Film Festival by Andy Warhol. 1967
Scene from Kubrick's *2001: A Space Odyssey.* 1968
The B.O.A.C. Concorde. From a 1968 advertisement
A Chorus Line. Photomontage by Paul Elsom/Martha Swope. © 1979

The Dreyfus Fund is a mutual investment fund in which the management hopes to make your money grow, and takes what it considers sensible risks in that direction. Your securities dealer or his mutual fund representative will be happy to give you a prospectus.

Dreyfus Fund. Ad. Lester Feldman. 1964. Dreyfus Fund Inc

Esso gasoline. Ad. Bob Jones. © 1965. Humble Oil & Refining Company

PUT A TIGER IN YOUR TANK!

MAKES EVEN '23's SKIDDOO!

If your car is feeling its age, give it a 3-way power boost with High-energy Esso Extra. It's the gasoline that: (1) cleans up fouled carburetors to restore lost power and mileage; (2) neutralizes harmful engine deposits to renew full firing power; (3) gives you the high octane for youthful performance. To bring power back alive, hunt for the Tiger . . . at the sign of *Happy Motoring!*

HUMBLE
OIL & REFINING COMPANY

. . . AMERICA'S LEADING ENERGY COMPANY . . . MAKERS OF ESSO PRODUCTS

ESSO

© HUMBLE OIL & REFINING COMPANY, 1965

The Equitable, life insurance. Ad. 1969.
The Equitable Life Assurance Society of the United States

"Mental retardation
ranks as a major
national health, social
and economic problem.
It strikes our most precio
asset, our children."

John F. Kennedy

Nothing was closer to the heart of John F. Kennedy than the health and welfare of America's children. But for one group he had an unusually deep and abiding concern — the mentally retarded.

Mental retardation handicaps 5½ million Americans. Every year 126,000 babies are born whose minds won't grow enough. Moreover, care of the retarded costs the nation billions of dollars annually.

Here are six things that you can do now to help prevent mental retardation and bring new hope to those whose minds are retarded:

1. If you expect a babe, stay under a doctor's or a hospital's care. Urge all expectant mothers to do so.

2. See that your schools have special teachers and special classes to identify and help mentally retarded children early in their lives.

3. Select jobs in your company that the mentally retarded can fill, and hire them.

4. Persuade employers to hire the mentally retarded and help those who cannot find work by themselves.

5. Accept the mentally retarded as American citizens. Give them a chance to live useful, dignified lives in your community.

6. Write for the free booklet to the President's Committee on Mental Retardation, Washington, D.C.

President's Committee on Mental Retardation. Ad.
(John F. Kennedy). 1965. Advertising Council Public Service

It doesn't take long for boys to find out it's a tough life. Fortunately, the people at Rhodes have known it for quite a while.

That's why they make shirts like these. First off, they're designed to match the way young guys move. Then, they're made of 100%. Acrilan* acrylic fiber. To keep their shape no matter what jams a fellow gets them into. (And color, no matter how many washings you put them through.)

To prove the point, we've Wear-Dated* them. That means they're guaranteed for a year's normal wear. (Return to Monsanto with tag and sales slip for refund or replacement.) Both styles come in twelve great colors. Sizes 6-20. Turtleneck model, about $3.50; fashion collar, about $5.

RHODES SAYS
THERE ARE NO BAD BOYS.
ONLY BAD SHIRTS.

Rhodes, boys' shirts. Ad. 1968. Rhodes Boyswear

My Fair Lady, Warner Brothers Pictures original sound track recording. Ad. 1964. Columbia Records

— C'est passionnant ce que vous lisez chérie ?....
— je vous crois! Le catalogue des vins Nicolas.....

Nicolas wines. Ad. Raymond Peynet. 1960. Etablissements Nicolas

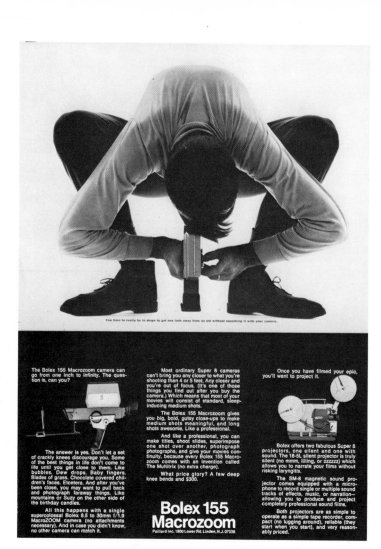

Bolex 155 Macrozoom camera. Ad. 1968. Paillard Inc

Don't stir without Noilly Prat. Ad. Lester Bookbinder.
1962. Browne-Vintners Company

For the Action Crowd...

New RCA VICTOR Portables with Solid Copper Circuit dependability

Your new "Pick of the Portables" can *take it—wherever* you take it—because every Sportabout TV gives you RCA Solid Copper Circuits. Solid Copper Circuits replace old-fashioned "hand wiring"—eliminate over 200 possible trouble spots. RCA Victor Solid Copper Circuits won't come loose and short circuit to cause service headaches. They're the circuits of the Space Age.

You get the sharpest, clearest pictures possible with these sharp new RCA Victor Sportabouts. They

"shift gears" electronically for greater picture-pulling power—a must for fringe area reception.

And remember: more people own RCA Victor than any other television, black and white or color. Shouldn't you?

 The Most Trusted Name in Electronics

RCA Victor Solid Copper Circuits are the circuits of the Space Age. They replace old-fashioned "hand wiring" in over 200 possible trouble spots . . . for greater dependability, better performance.

New RCA Victor Portables. Ad. 1965. RCA Corporation

The
tip
that's
setting
the
trend

Bachelor cigarettes. Ad. Lester Bookbinder. 1962. John Player & Sons

Make today a Heinz Souperday

If you spent 40 days in the sun you'd be rosy and plump, too.

Hunt's tomatoes spend their lives lolling in the sun. Then when they have a nice color, are firm and vine-ripened, we stuff as many as two pounds of them into each bottle of Hunt's Catsup.

Hunt's CATSUP

So the catsup is thick, rich with big tomato taste. There's nothing like a well-rested tomato to make a lively catsup. **HUNT-WESSON FOODS** FULLERTON, CALIFORNIA

Hunt's Catsup. Ad. Lynn St John. 1968. Hunt-Wesson Foods, Inc

TOP:
Heinz soups. Poster. John Crewe. 1968. H. J. Heinz Company Ltd

RIGHT:
Lea & Perrins Sauce. Ad. Richard Jeffery. 1971. Lea & Perrins, Inc

There's no Worcestershire like an old Worcestershire.

An older Worcestershire makes a wiser stew. (To say nothing of a brighter burger, smarter salad, loftier meatloaf.)

And by older Worcestershire, we can be talking only about Lea & Perrins, the Worcestershire that's aged in wood, like fine wine, and mellowed to perfection, like good steak and cheese. The Worcestershire that combines natural aging with natural ingredients—things like eschalots, tamarinds, anchovies and chili peppers—to bring out the best in every dish.

The Worcestershire, in short, that's seasoned right to start with and seasoned even better with age.

Lea & Perrins. The More Seasoned Worcestershire.

FAMILY FOOD IDEAS

Cooking is Child's play in the November Family Circle.

In her own warm, wonderful style, TV's Julia Child tells ways you can get more pleasure out of preparing meals. Also on the November menu:

(A) NEW SPEED KNITTING. Handsome hand-knits appearing exclusively in Family Circle. And you can knit any one of them in just a few hours! **(B) THANKSGIVING TURKEY DINNER.** A whole flock of new ideas for making Thanksgiving dinner an occasion to remember. **(C) BEAUTY: EVENING MAKE-UP.** New ways to look your best at night. **(D) LITTLE TABLES YOU CAN MAKE.** Do-it-yourself cocktail and coffee tables to enhance your living room. **(E) CRAFTS:** MARVELOUS MINIATURES. Crazy, fun-to-make gifts. **(F) PILLOW TOYS YOU CAN MAKE.** Kids will go wild over them!

Also for November: How to Talk to Teens About Sex, by **Sloan Wilson.** And the beginning of a new regular feature by **Dr. Rose Franzblau,** leading authority on family living and children— exclusively for Family Circle readers.

It's all in the November Family Circle— read it and save time and money.

Check out the November Family Circle. At your supermarket, now.

Family Circle, a publication of Cowles Communications. Title Reg. U.S. Pat. Off., ©1967, The Family Circle, Inc.

66 LOOK 10-31-67

Family Circle magazine. Ad. © 1967. The Family Circle Inc

OVERLEAF: Hertz, car rentals. Ad. 1962. The Hertz Corporation

Before you fly off on vacation, call Hertz—and a clean new Chevrolet or other fine car will meet you at the airport or anywhere under the sun!

mething!

he driver's seat!

HERTZ
RENT A CAR

Salvador Dali—from the Lenthéric Collection

It began with a dream of women. Women in all their infinite variety. We were haunted by that dream. And so we sought out twelve of the world's great painters and said to them: "Women. What do you see in them? Paint for us your version, your vision of their very essence."

Some painted the colors of their laughter. Others captured the trembling of an unshed tear. Some saw their sunlight. Others felt their secret silences.

Then one day, the paintings were ours. To draw from. To distill. To extend presence into perfume. A perfume all mood, all magic, all wonder, all woman. This is how Lenthéric 12 happened. Now let it happen to you.

LENTHÉRIC 12 *A portrait in perfume*

Lenthéric 12 perfume. Ad. Salvador Dali. 1962.
Lenthéric Inc

Metropolitan Opera. Poster. Marc Chagall. 1966.
Lincoln Center for the Performing Arts and
the American Federation of Arts

Private Showing—and V.O. enhances the occasion with its flawless flavor and genuine talent for pleasing particular people.

KNOWN BY THE COMPANY IT KEEPS **SEAGRAM'S**

VO
IMPORTED
CANADIAN WHISKY

Seagram's VO Imported Canadian Whiskey. Ad. 1961.
Seagram-Distillers Company

Cannes. Poster. Pablo Picasso. 1963. French National Tourist Office

MONET, MASTER JEWELER, CREATES THE "VALENCIENNE" COLLECTION. NECKLACE, $25. MATCHING EARRINGS, $15. BRACELET, NOT SHOWN, $12.50. PLUS TAX. AT THE FINEST STORES.

jewelry in the golden manner of Monet

Monet jewelry. Ad. 1964. Altman/Stoller. Monet Jewelers Inc

VOGUE

75¢
MAY

LOOK
LIKE
A BEAUTY
THIS
SUMMER:
THE CHANGES,
THE FACTS,
THE FUN

RACY
NEW
FASHIONS
FOR THE
SUMMER-
ACTION...
NEW WIT
AND LUXE
FOR THE
BEACH LIFE

Vogue magazine. Cover. Irving Penn. 1964. The Condé Nast Publications Inc

Gubelin jewelry. Ad (detail). 1960. Gubelin, Lucerne

'Meet the Beatles!' Album cover. Robert Freeman.
1963. Capital Records Inc

258

Top Cat. Poster. Peter Max. 1967. Peter Max Enterprises

Step Through the Looking-Glass Into...

Douglas DC8 jetliners. Ad. Tirce. 1965.
Douglas Aircraft Co

This is the first Christmas card, but

this English holiday greeting is older!

When J. C. Horsley designed the first Christmas card in 1843, Gordon's Gin had already been an English holiday fixture for 74 years. Obviously, then, you're on very firm traditional ground when you give a gift of Gordon's. Nice thing is, Gordon's still harks back to Alexander Gordon's original 1769 formula, which keeps it distinctively dry and flavoursome. So your gift is not only richly historical, it tastes good, too. Ideal Christmas gift, wouldn't you say?

Gordon's Distilled London Dry Gin. Ad. Paccione.
1963. Gordon's Dry Gin Company Ltd

London Hilton. Ad. 1964.
Hilton International Ltd

go English eat at the London Tavern

at the sign of the turtle—400 years of english cooking tradition

Outside the London Tavern in the London Hilton you'll see a turtle emblem. What's going on behind his back? It isn't cricket. They're making turtle soup. And they're doing wonderful things to pigeons too. The London Tavern has done more than just adopt the name of a mid-sixteenth century establishment. It has adopted the best of its culinary traditions. You can't see, as you could in the 18th century, two tons of live turtles swimming in an open tank, but you can see and sample a hearty menu that is uncompromisingly *English*. In the quiet cool greens and browns of the countryside you can choose from the Spit and Grate, the Cold Larder, the Copper Wagon, the Tavern Roast. There's Porterhouse Steak, Lord Derby's Irish Stew, Loin of Berkshire Pork, Green Melon Flummery, Banbury Apple in Crust, and John Farley's Pigeon Pie. And English ale by the half-pint, pint and yard. For reservations, ring HYDe Park 8000 and ask for the London Tavern.   **GO INTERNATIONAL—STAY HILTON**

LONDON HILTON

HILTON HOTELS IN
Berlin · Cairo · Madrid
Amsterdam · Rotterdam
Athens · Istanbul
Tehran · Rome
Also in the Caribbean, the Pacific, Latin America and in 39 cities in the United States. Ring the Hilton Reservation Service at Hyde Park 8000 to make immediate reservations at any Hilton Hotel anywhere in the world, or contact your travel agent.

Why do well-traveled people travel Sabena? People who go places find that Sabena's 3-speed fleet is going their way, at just the time they want. For instance: you make the first big jump by Boeing "Intercontinental"; jet on around Europe by Caravelle; slow down for the unique experience of "Flight-Seeing"... by helicopter. Next trip to Europe, Africa, the Middle East ... fly Sabena. All the way, le service Belgique – c'est magnifique!

Ask your Travel Agent to book you aboard Sabena's 3-speed fleet...or call Sabena Belgian World Airlines. More than 200 offices in the principal cities of the world.

Sabena. Ad. 1961. Sabena Belgian World Airlines

New England Life, insurance. Ad. Rowland B. Wilson.
© 1969. New England Mutual Life Insurance Company

Take a trip to Lotus Land. Mailing poster for Push Pin
Studios. Milton Glaser. 1968. Push Pin Studios

Neiman-Marcus, department store. Ad. Dorothy Michaelson.
1967. Neiman-Marcus Co., Dallas

When the tag goes on
it will read
NUPRON.
MODULIZED™ RAYON

Nupron Modulized rayon lives! It does the knit bit like it's never been done before. It breathes
life into blends, textures and colors. It inspires freedom in styling and dressing. It gives comfort and carefreeness
wherever it goes. In short, it promises you the world. So don't let it pass you by. C'mon out in
Nupron Modulized rayon. Live like you've never lived before.

Nupron Modulized rayon, a product of I-R-C Fibers Division, Midland-Ross, is made from highly purified and specialized grades of
chemical cellulose produced by ITT Rayonier Incorporated, a subsidiary of International Telephone & Telegraph Corporation, New York, N.Y.

Nupron Modulized Rayon. Ad. Charles Santore/Dick Herdigan. ITT Rayonier Incorporated

Smirnoff Vodka. Ad (Woody Allen, Monique Van Vooren, Charles Reid, Julie Newmar, 'Killer' Joe Piro, and Dolores Hawkins). 1966. Ste. Pierre Smirnoff, Fls. Inc

Martini & Rossi vermouth. Ad. Bert Stern. 1969. Renfield Importers Ltd

IS! GIVE A SMIRNOFF MULE PARTY

o host and the smart drink to serve. For a cool, refreshing Mule, made with Up®, is a drink you can start with and stay with all evening. Only crystal filtered through 14,000 pounds of activated charcoal, blends so perfectly t's why there's only one rule for the Mule. *Make it with Smirnoff!*

HOW TO MAKE THE SMIRNOFF MULE Jigger of Smirnoff over ice. Add juice of ½ lime. Fill Mule mug or glass with 7-Up to taste. Delicious! **Set of 6 Mule mugs—$3.00.** Send check or money order to Smirnoff Mule, Dept. A, P. O. Box 225, Brooklyn, N.Y. 11202. Allow 30 days for delivery.

Always ask for *Smirnoff* **VODKA** *It leaves you breathless®*

80 AND 100 PROOF. DISTILLED FROM GRAIN. STE PIERRE SMIRNOFF FLS. (DIVISION OF HEUBLEIN), HARTFORD, CONN.

Are you a Top Grade nut nut?

Are you the kind of nut who's nuts about the taste of top rank, top notch, top grade nuts?
Then stand easy and hear this:
A truly top nut is the U. S. Grade No. 1 peanut. (Saluted everywhere as the "nut nut's nut.")
Only two things give you the fine,

fresh-roasted flavor of fancy U. S. Grade No. 1 peanuts. Peanuts themselves and Skippy Peanut Butter. Skippy® is peanuts— No. 1 Peanuts in their most spreadable, edible form.
And because of the secret patented way it's made, only Skippy captures and keeps

that elusive, fresh-roasted flavor for you— right down to the last delicious dab.
So, whether you rank as a nut nut or not, the fact is
if you like peanuts— you'll like Skippy. America's top-selling peanut butter.

Skippy, peanut butter. Ad. 1967. Corn Products Co

Some Volkswagen owners look down on other Volkswagen owners.

When you graduate from a Volkswagen Sedan to a Volkswagen Station Wagon, you really step up in the world.

The Station Wagon stands a good foot taller than other cars.

And it holds more than the biggest conventional wagon you can find.

But the VW Wagon isn't only tall.

It's also short.

We saved 4 feet of hood in front by putting the engine in back.

Big as it is inside, it's only 9 inches longer than the Volkswagen Sedan.

So people who move up to the high-slung model still feel very much at home.

They park in the same little spots.

They still don't worry about freezing or boiling; the engine is air-cooled.

They still go a long way on a gallon of gas (about 24 miles) and a very long way on a set of tires (about 30,000 miles).

And it just tickles them to drive one Volkswagen and look down on a million others.

Volkswagen. Ad. © 1963. Volkswagen of America Inc

"I backed our car over the suitcase. Inside was my husband's portable radio..."

"I got so rattled, I put the car in drive and ran over it again." American Tourister knows that for a suitcase, a lot of trips aren't exactly a pleasure.

So we put sixteen different strong materials into every case we build. We give American Touristers a tough stainless steel frame. And nonspring locks that won't spring open on impact. And fiber glass reinforcement. All over. Not just on the corners. All of which does more than protect our suitcase. It protects what's inside our suitcase.

"My heart was in my mouth, but the radio wasn't even scratched.

It works perfectly."

Could that ordinary suitcase of yours take on a 4100 lb. car? Could it survive crashing over the side of an ocean liner? Or bouncing from a car doing 70 mph?

Try it. We'd be delighted to know what happens.

"I thought your American Tourister luggage held up remarkably well." Mrs. J. Chris Swift Columbia, S.C.

American Tourister

Vintage Year?

The maturing of good wine is a process which cannot be hurried. Likewise with MG. 40 years of steady development and enthusiasm have gone into the making of today's Midget. The Mk II Sports Convertible has fully wind-up windows and adjustable quarter lights, lockable doors with exterior handles, curved windscreen, new suspension, increased power, new de luxe cockpit plus the vast resources of B.M.C.

Safety Fast MG MIDGET Mk.II Sports Convertible £623.17.1. (inc. £106.17.1. P.T.)

MG Midget. Ad. 1964. British Motor Corporation

American Tourister suitcases. Ad. Dick Stone. 1966. American Luggage Works Inc

Ford's Cortina. Ad (detail). 1969. Ford Motor Co

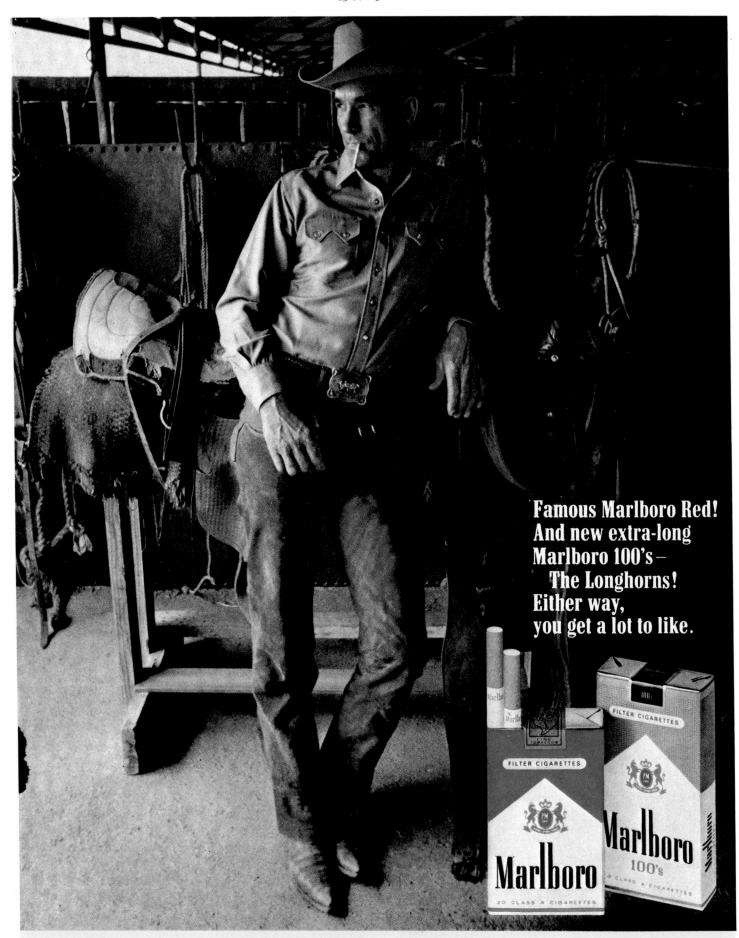

Famous Marlboro Red!
And new extra-long
Marlboro 100's –
The Longhorns!
Either way,
you get a lot to like.

Come to where the flavor is. Come to Marlboro Country.

Marlboro cigarettes. Ad. Art Kane. 1967. Philip Morris & Co., Inc

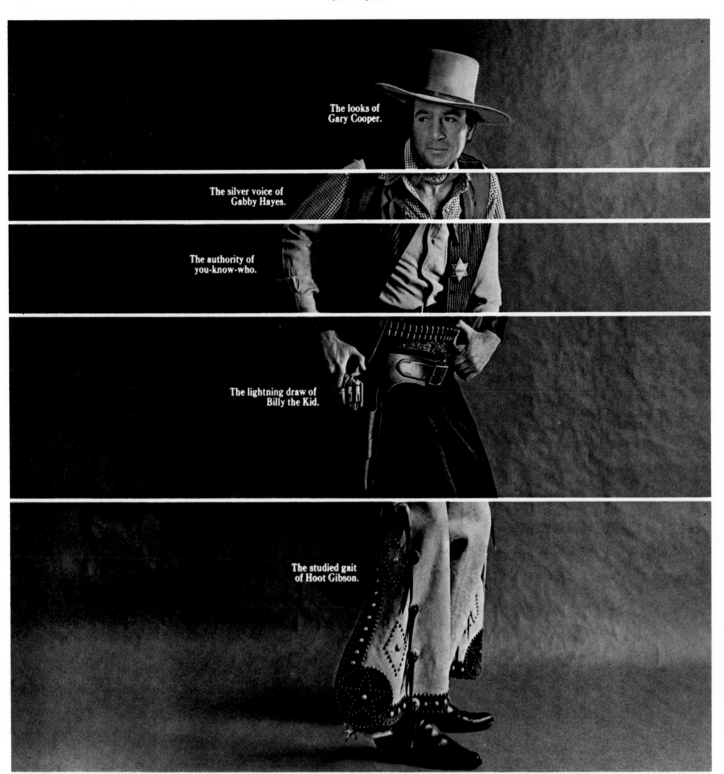

The looks of
Gary Cooper.

The silver voice of
Gabby Hayes.

The authority of
you-know-who.

The lightning draw of
Billy the Kid.

The studied gait
of Hoot Gibson.

The Super Cowboy:

We put one together to show you how we made our Scotch.

We were after the smoothest shots ever to come out of Scotland. Macallan, Cardow, Tain, Glenlossie, Keith and the other greats. These prize whiskies form the base of the world's greatest Scotches. Most distillers settle for 1 or 2 key whiskies and round out their blends with other fine whiskies. It took more than 20 years to collect ours. But now you can try the world's greatest Scotches all at once simply by having a showdown at any friendly "saloon."

100 PIPERS
Scotch by Seagram

EVERY DROP BOTTLED IN SCOTLAND · SELECTED AND IMPORTED BY SEAGRAM-DISTILLERS COMPANY, N.Y.C. · BLENDED SCOTCH WHISKY · 86 PROOF

100 Pipers Scotch by Seagram. Ad. William Helburn. 1967. Seagram Distillers Company

Hair, musical. Poster. Ruspoli-Rodriguez. © 1968. National Productions

Travel advertisement. 1963. Transworld Airlines, Paris

USA?
TWA!

Las Vegas — un océan de lumière sur le ciel du désert! Des orchestres
réputés. Des meneurs de jeu célèbres dans le monde entier. Des rires.
De l'animation! Entrez dans la danse quand vous voudrez. Et pour être
de la fête voyagez TWA — la seule compagnie aérienne qui conduit de
Paris aux USA et y dessert 70 villes. Préparez votre voyage avec la
brochure gratuite de TWA "Bonnes Vacances USA", et vous écono-
miserez de l'argent! *Adressez-vous à votre Agent de Voyages ou à TWA.*

U.S.A · Europe
Africa · Asia
depend on

THE ELECTRIC CIRCUS
THE ULTIMATE LEGAL ENTERTAINMENT EXPERIENCE

SAINT MARKS PLACE, BETWEEN 2ND & 3RD, EAST VILLAGE, N.Y.C.

"TM" ® © 1967 Electric Circus of New York, inc. Pat. Pend. Coffee in the Third Eye."

Printed in U.S.A.

Bob Dylan, folk singer. Poster, inserted in a record. Milton Glaser. 1966. Push Pin Studios
The Electric Circus. Poster. Jacqui Morgan. © 1967. Electric Circus of New York

Piper champagne. Ad. Charles van Mannen. 1968.
Renfield Importers Ltd

Advertisement for bookbinding materials (detail).
Ralph Dobson. 1962. Grange Fibre Co., Ltd

Hello Dolly, motion picture. Album cover.
Pen & Pencil Creative Services. © 1969.
20th Century-Fox Record Corporation

Glass etchings by New Zealander John Hutton, who has also designed glass panels for the Coventry and Guildford Cathedrals.

Stratford

Levi Fox talks Birthdays

"Shakespeare belongs to the world now. And the world has responded marvellously to his 400th birthday. The Shakespeare Centre, the permanent memorial, can be called a birthday present from the world: Gifts come in daily. The spirit here is terribly exciting. All the art and decoration produced is modern—alive and very much a part of today. This year, we can influence the way people think about—and study —the man. The door is completely open; we've got the whole world with us." Mr. Levi Fox, M.A.,F.S.A., F.R. Hist.S., F.R.S., is Director & Secretary of the Shakespeare Birthday Trust.

A FEW MORE FACTS. The season runs to December. Plays: Richard II, Henry IV, part 1, Henry IV, part 2, Henry V, Henry VI, Edward IV, and Richard III.

Stratford also offers the Shakespeare Exhibition this year, plus lectures, poetry recitals, music concerts, films, folk dancing. Stratford . . on the road to 1564. And BP? On all roads to Stratford.

BP IS THE KEY TO BETTER MOTORING **BP** *(AND TO SEEING BETTER FESTIVALS, TOO)*

BP. Ad. John Hutton (glass etchings). 1964. British-Petroleum Co., Ltd

Your computer is a monster?

Everybody loves a big, shiny, new computer.

At first.

But if it can't do all you want it to . . .

If jobs take longer than you were told they would . . .

If all of a sudden you need a lot of expensive extras . . .

You might very well decide you've got a monster in your computer room.

So how do you avoid it?

You make sure your computer com-

pany takes the time and trouble to really understand your problems.

You don't accept any pat solutions if your problems are un-pat.

You talk to the other computer company in the first place.

The Other Computer Company:

Honeywell

Sculpture by Jack N. Rindner

Honeywell computers. Ad. Jack Rindner (sculpture). 1969. Honeywell Inc

Otis elevators. Ad (detail). Arnold Beckerman. 1969. Otis Elevator Company

Philco television. Ad. N.A.S.A. 1969. Philco-Ford
Corporation

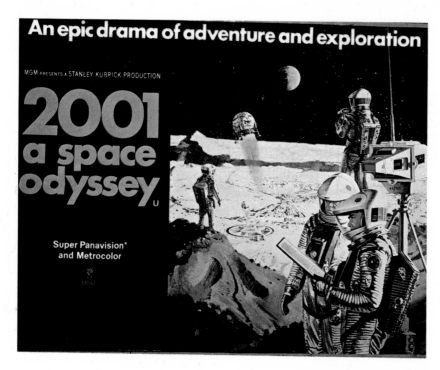

2001: A Space Odyssey, motion picture. Poster. 1968.
MGM

We Reach the Moon. Ad. 1969. The New York Times/
Bantam Books Inc

Moonship: General Dynamics technology. Ad (detail). Peter Turner. 1969. General Dynamics Communication Co

Jesus Christ Superstar, musical; recording. Poster.
David Edward Byrd. 1971. Decca Records

TOP LEFT:
Stop Pollution. Poster. Jacqueline S. Casey. 1970.
Massachusetts Institute of Technology

LEFT:
Follies, musical. Poster. David Edward Byrd. 1970.
Winter Garden Theatre

Life Is So Beautiful: anti-smoking poster (detail). Peter Max. 1972. American Cancer Society Inc

© 1979 Dan River Inc., Apparel Fabrics Marketing Division, 111 West 40th St., N.Y. 10018 Tel./212-554-5632.

Dan River's stretch corduroy can g

No stress, no strain with our happy blend of cotton, Dacron polyester and Lycra spandex. Bec

DISCO

...ou into some pretty tight spots.

River knows how to ease the squeeze. **Dan River Runs Deep**

Dan River fabric. Ad. Gerry Weinman. © 1979. Dan River Inc

283

Cannon Royal Classic Towel. Ad. Ron Harris. 1979.
Cannon Mills Inc

Pioneer, mini system. Ad. Derek Seagram. 1979.
Pioneer High Fidelity (GB) Ltd

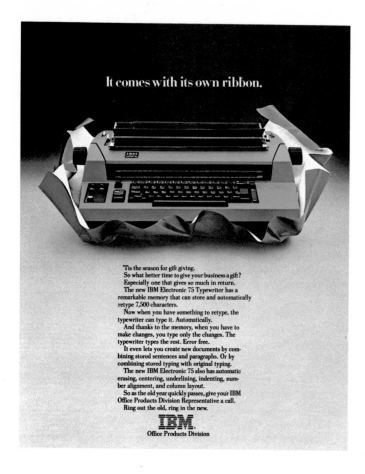

The New IBM Electronic 75 Typewriter. Ad. Hunter Freeman.
1979. International Business Machines Corp

Habitat. Ad. Dick Kruger. 1978. Kohler Co

3000 tuner, the CT-3000 cassette deck and the PL-3000 turntable, linked with details of the Pioneer Privilege Purchase Plan, a very low interest credit scheme. **EVERYTHING YOU HEAR IS TRUE.**   ⊘**PIONEER**®

Energy operations annual report cover. Fred Otnes. 1979. Mobil Corporation

British Steel enterprises. Ad. Brian Buselle. 1974.
British Steel Corporation

Xerox 9400 duplicator. Ad. Michael Raab. 1977.
Xerox Corporation

Aurea jewelry. Ad. Cosimo. 1979.
Aurea Jewelry Creations Inc

"In the presence of the Great White... time suspends itself."
Peter Benchley

Few moments rival the excitement of meeting a Great White Shark face to face. For Peter Benchley, author of *Jaws*, survival depends on experience and precision equipment. Peter wears the gold Rolex Submariner. This Oyster Perpetual, an officially certified superlative chronometer, is carved out of a solid block of 18 kt. gold (1680/9290) $3,825. Also available in stainless steel (1680/9315) $490. Write for free brochure, Rolex Watch U.S.A., Inc., Rolex Bldg., 665 Fifth Ave., N.Y., N.Y. 10022.

ROLEX

Rolex chronometer. Ad. T. Walker Lloyd. 1976. Rolex Watch U.S.A., Inc

World Wildlife Fund. Poster. S. N. Surti. 1975. Air-India

'Join the Family.' Poster (detail). Richard and Mark Hess. 1979. Minnesota Zoological Society

The Ritz hotel. Ad. Ken Gilliam. 1980.
The Ritz, London

Burberrys' weathercoat. Ad. Lord Lichfield. 1979.
Burberrys Ltd

Aquascutum coats. Ad. Gene Vernier. 1973.
Aquascutum of London

Put away a little gold for a rainy day.

EVERY PACKET CARRIES A GOVERNMENT HEALTH WARNING

Benson and Hedges' Special Filter cigarettes. Ad. Julian Cottrell. 1973. Benson and Hedges

Take it from the manufacturer.

Wool. It's worth more. Naturally.

American Wool Council

Dept. WW-280, 200 Clayton Street
Denver, CO 80206

Take it from the manufacturer. Ad. 1980. American Wool Council

Reproduced from the original unretouched photograph.

You remember the
fun with instant pictures.

Simulated television picture.

The story o
(Or how to remembe

The photograph above is a dramatization of something that actually happened.

We wanted to tell you how real we think the picture is on Sylvania color television.

Of course, GTE Sylvania engineers would

be happy to do so. Likewise our dealers. And set owners too.

But they could be biased. Besides, we wanted to do it in a way you'd remember.

We did. In a dramatization that's on the

air now.

It's a commercial (if you hav that starts with a cat at an open

He's looking into a room in w a canary is being shown on a

Simulated picture.

You relive it all with Polaroid's instant motion pictures.

onder and excitement of instant movies! So easy to
it aim and shoot. Then pop the cassette into the player,
n or projector to set up, and seconds later all the color

and action is back. Save a little of today for tomorrow. Polavision
is more than an instant movie. It's a living diary of your family.
For more information, call us collect: 617-864-1534.

Polavision. Instant movies from Polaroid.

©Polaroid Corporation 1979. "Polaroid" and "Polavision"®

730 Third Ave., New York 10017

nd the canary.

e can look on color television.)

on set.
nds there watching the film . . .
wing with the movement of the
e screen.
drops to the floor. Slowly, as if

stalking his prey, he starts toward the set.
As the cat nears the set he stops. Snarls.
And then . . . springs.
We hope you'll remember this little drama-
tization when you're out shopping for a color

television set.
Especially if you want a really real-looking
picture. **GTE SYLVANIA**
a part of General Telephone & Electronics

America's Favorite Cigarette Break.

Benson & Hedges 100's.

Regular & Menthol. 21 mg. "tar," 1.4 mg. nicotine av. per cigarette, FTC Report, Aug. '71.

Benson & Hedges 100's. Ad. Steve Horn. 1971.
Philip Morris & Co., Inc

TOP LEFT:
Polavision, instant movies. Ad. Harold Krieger. © 1979.
Polaroid Corporation

LEFT:
Sylvania, color television. Ad. Menkin Seltzer. 1971.
General Telephone & Electronics Corporation

Talk to a Scots shepherd whose family has lived near Stirling Castle for 600 years.

Talking to anyone in Scotland is easy. Getting there and getting around is easy too. For example, fly direct to Prestwick in Scotland. Hire a car for only $40 for the week.

Ask about the legend that says Mary Queen of Scots still walks the castle battlements.

Another quaint legend says everyone everywhere in Europe speaks English. They don't.

Agree that Mary's ghost might be the reason the local inn stocks 24 different blends of whisky.

In Scotland whisky means Scotch. And a way of life. Ask for unblended Glenlivet. Experts say it's the best.

Inquire how to get to the inn nearby.

Bed and breakfast (juice, porridge, kippers, eggs, rashers of bacon, rolls, toast, milk as rich as cream, cream as thick as butter, and butter like nothing you've ever tasted) plus coffee or tea only $5.25.

Question the chambermaid about whether Scotsmen really do wear the kilt.

As ingenious an excuse to talk to a pretty girl as we ever heard.

Understand everybody because everybody understands you.

We speak your language England, Northern Ireland, Scotland, Wales.

For your free 52-page booklet, "Vacations in Britain 1971", see your travel agent or cut out this line, fill in your Name_____
and Address_____Zip_____and mail to: British Tourist Authority, Dept. LS, Box 4100, New York, N.Y. 10017.

Travel advertisement. Alfred Eisenstaedt. 1971. British Tourist Authority

Medaillon, cognac. Ad. Adrian Flowers. 1979. Martell & Co

Among photographers Adrian Flowers has been known as the master-craftsman for over 20 years. His work has won awards in a multitude of fields. From magazine editorial, to special assignments for the Museum of Mankind. By his choosing to photograph a fine VSOP like Medaillon Liqueur Cognac, you can guess what his favourite subjects have been: The beautiful, and the rare.

MARTELL. THE FAMILY OF COGNAC SINCE 1715.

WHAT ADRIAN FLOWERS THINKS OF MEDAILLON.

Agatha Christie novel. Ad (detail). Fred Otnes. 1976. Doubleday & Co., Inc

Heaven Can Wait, motion picture. Poster. 1979.
Birney Lettick. Paramount Pictures

Upstairs, Downstairs, television program. Ad.
Ivan Chermayeff. 1976. Mobil Oil Corporation

White Shoulders perfume. Ad. Howell Conant. 1976. Evyan Perfumes, Inc

Rainbow necklace. Ad (detail). Pamplemousse. 1979. Boucheron

BMW motorcycle. Ad. 1973. BMW Park Lane

The Great Escape

A BMW motorcycle offers what no car can: an exhilaration that only first-hand proximity to elements and surroundings can bring. The excitement of close contact with wind and sun that blows free business cares and boardroom blues; awakens nostalgic memories of days when two wheels took you far and fast.

And a BMW offers what no other motorcycle can: a combination of the confidence and dependability of sophisticated BMW engineering; a drive shaft to unchain the engine's smooth riding potential; horizontal twin engine for perfect balance and cooling; electric starter to eliminate kick-start gymnastics*; double-cam brakes (the hotter they get, the harder they grip); and extra-long-reach telescopic forks to dampen the bumps but not the fun. Add a BMW motorcycle to your garage. And get a lot more fun out of life! *Optional on the R50/5.

BMW – the finest motorcycles in the World

Where to view and test ride a BMW motorcycle:

John Ace (Garages) Ltd Swansea.
Tel: Swansea 53163
Black and White Garages Ltd
Harvington, Worcs. Tel: Harvington 612
Comerfords Thames Ditton, Surrey.
Tel: 01-398 5531
Chas Coombe Ltd Slough.
Tel: Slough 22354
Chas E Cope & Sons Ltd
Smethwick, Worcs.
Tel: Smethwick 3501
Dowsons Scarborough Garage
Tel: Scarborough 64361
Harry Fairbairn Ltd Irvine, Ayrshire.
Tel: Irvine 472793

Frosfield Service Station
Petersfield, Hants. Tel: Hawkley 200
Victor Horsman Ltd Liverpool.
Tel: 051-709 9944
Ken Heanes Ltd Fleet, Hants.
Tel: Fleet 7673
Allan Jefferies Ltd Shipley, Yorks.
Tel: Shipley 54271
Kingsworthy Motors Winchester.
Tel: Winchester 68333/4
Gus Kuhn Ltd London, SW9.
Tel: 01-733 1002/3/4
Dick Lovett Specialist Cars
Wroughton, Wilts.
Tel: Wroughton 812387

Lazenby Garages Ltd
Rothley, Leics. Tel: Rothley 2484
Mill Garages (Sunderland) Ltd
Tel: Sunderland 57631/2/3
Devick Motique Ltd Long Eaton,
Derbs. Tel: Long Eaton 3578
Reliance of Chingford Ltd
Chingford, Essex. Tel: 01-527 5057
Revetts (Norwich Road) Ltd
Ipswich. Tel: Ipswich 53726
Queens Park Motors Ltd
Manchester. Tel: 061-736 3514/2585
Read Bros (Cycles) Ltd
Leytonstone. Tel: 01-539 1383
Slocombe's Ltd NW10. 01-450 8655

Two Wheel Services Ltd
Bridgend, Glamorgan.
Tel: Bridgend 5496
Tintern Garage Tintern, Mons.
Tel: Tintern 344
Rob Walker Ltd New Milton,
Hants. Tel: New Milton 611133
Western Counties Automobile
Co Ltd Bristol. Tel: Bristol 45561
Williams Motor Co Ltd
Manchester. Tel: 061-832 8781/6
A Williams & Co Cheltenham,
Tel: Cheltenham 56281
Whittakers Motors Ltd
Blackpool. Tel: Blackpool 24828

PRE-VAT PRICE REDUCTIONS APPLICABLE NOW CAN SAVE YOU UP TO £150!
Special Pre-Vat reductions valid until April 1st: BMW R50.5 (500cc) £899.01. R60 5 (600cc)
£999.30 or the BMW R75 5 (750cc) £1147.93 Prices shown are rec. retail prices including P.T.
For full details and Literature on the BMW motorcycle range send this coupon to:
Motorcycle Marketing Division
BMW House, Chiswick High Road, London W4
Telephone: 01-995 4651

Name
Address

London Showroom, N.A.T.O. Diplomatic and Export Office, 56 Park Lane, London W.1. Telephone 01-499 6881.

Hathaway turns its hand to seawear.

You see merely the tip of the iceberg. Just a sampling of a spanking new collection from Hathaway.

The shirts, like signal flags fluttering from halyards, make bright splashes of color; among them, such hues as orange and green and flaring yellow. Every shirt is the very plushest of cotton terry cloths.

In the matter of trousers and jackets, Hathaway has chosen to avoid the obvious fabrics. Instead, it has used a soft yet rugged canvas twill in a natural shade that contrasts with the vividness of the shirts.

The boat shorts are of canvas, too, double-pleated and cuffed and rigged with a flapped coin pocket.

The jacket is but one of three, each cut from bolts of pure cotton canvas twill. Not shown, a pullover jacket with a big kangaroo pocket in front. And another fitted with a snap-off hood.

This, then, is seawear. Casual things to wear while knocking around in boats or backyards. From those Yankee craftsmen at the C.F. Hathaway Co., up in Waterville, Maine.

Hathaway seaware. Ad. Bob Stone. 1980. C. F. Hathaway Co

We build grip into all our car tyres.

Grand Prix racing drivers trust Goodyear technology to give them grip. So can you. When you drive on G800+S. Supersteel.

The steel-belted radial car tyre built to give you grip in bad weather. Extra high mileage too. Drive on G800+S. Supersteel.

Tyre technology from Goodyear.

G800+S. Supersteel.

GOODYEAR
The Choice of Champions.

Goodyear tyres. Ad. David Phipps. 1977.
Goodyear Tyre & Rubber Company (GB) Ltd

Made with Antron III DuPont registered trademark. Cup: All "Antron III" Nylon. Cupfill: All "Kodel" Polyester. Back: "Antron" Nylon, Nylon, "Lycra" Spandex. Exclusive of decoration. Prices are suggested retail. Coat by Daniel Hechter. Shoes by LaMarca.

The Maidenform Woman. Ad. Chris Von Wangenheim. 1980. Maidenform Inc

LOOK

Available at:
Abraham & Straus
Ann Taylor
Bamberger's
Benhil
Bloomingdale's
Bullock's
Burdines
Davison's, Atlanta
Emporium, San Francisco
Filene's
G. Fox
Gimbels
Macy's, Kansas City
Macy's, New York
Joseph Magnin, San Francisco
Jordan Marsh, Florida
Saks Fifth Avenue (Early On Shop)
& other fine stores

Jordache Designer Jeans. Ad. Hank Londoner. 1979. Jordache Enterprises Inc

The Homecoming, play. Poster. John J. Sorbie. 1973.
Johnson Hall Theatre

Under the Sun, ballet. Poster. Alexander Calder. 1976. The Pennsylvania Ballet

New York City Ballet Stravinsky Festival. Poster.
Don Matus. 1972. City Center of Music & Drama Inc

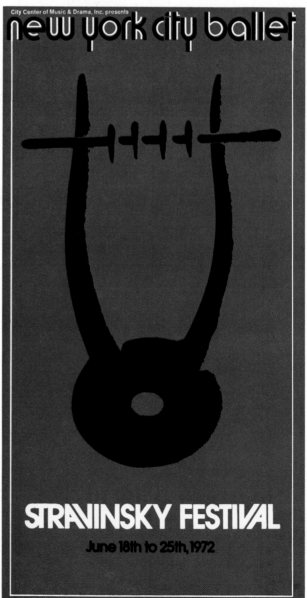

VOGUE
PARIS

DÉC./JAN. F 30

PAR

MIRÓ

Vogue magazine (Paris). Cover. Joan Miró. 1979. Les Editions Condé Nast SA

'No Nukes', on Asylum Records and Tapes. Ad. © 1979. A. Warner Communications Co

Star Trek (Paramount Pictures), recording on Columbia Records and Tapes. Ad. Maxine Smart. © 1979. CBS Inc

Weil de Weil. Created in France, the country that created Paris.

Weil de Weil perfume. Ad. © 1976.
Weil Parfumeur, Paris Inc

The French have
always known how to make your
heart beat a little faster.

Le Bikini 1954.......!

Vionnet 1921 – one of the first great
French haute couture designers – she created
for all the fashionable ladies of the decade.

Hennessy Cognac.
First started hearts beating
a little faster in 1765.

Hennessy Cognac. Ad. Roger Vionnet/Roy Giles/James
Cotterell. 1973. IDV Home Trade Ltd

Danskins, tights and sweater legs. Ad. Richard Davis.
1979. Danskin Inc

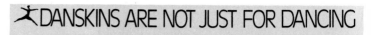

DANSKINS ARE NOT JUST FOR DANCING

SAVE ENERGY. WEAR DANSKINS. OUR LEG-WARMING TIGHTS AND SWEATER LEGS KEEP YOUR SPIRITS HIGH WHEN THE THERMOSTAT'S LOW. KEEP
YOU LOOKING GREAT ALL THE TIME. IN BULKY KNIT ORLON, RIBBED COTTON, TWEEDS, THERMAL TERRY, REGULAR NYLON AND MORE. AT FINE
STORES. OR SEND $1.00 FOR OUR FULL COLOR BROCHURE TO DANSKIN, INC., BOX 844, TIMES SQUARE STATION, T 12, NEW YORK, N.Y. 10036.
DANSKIN

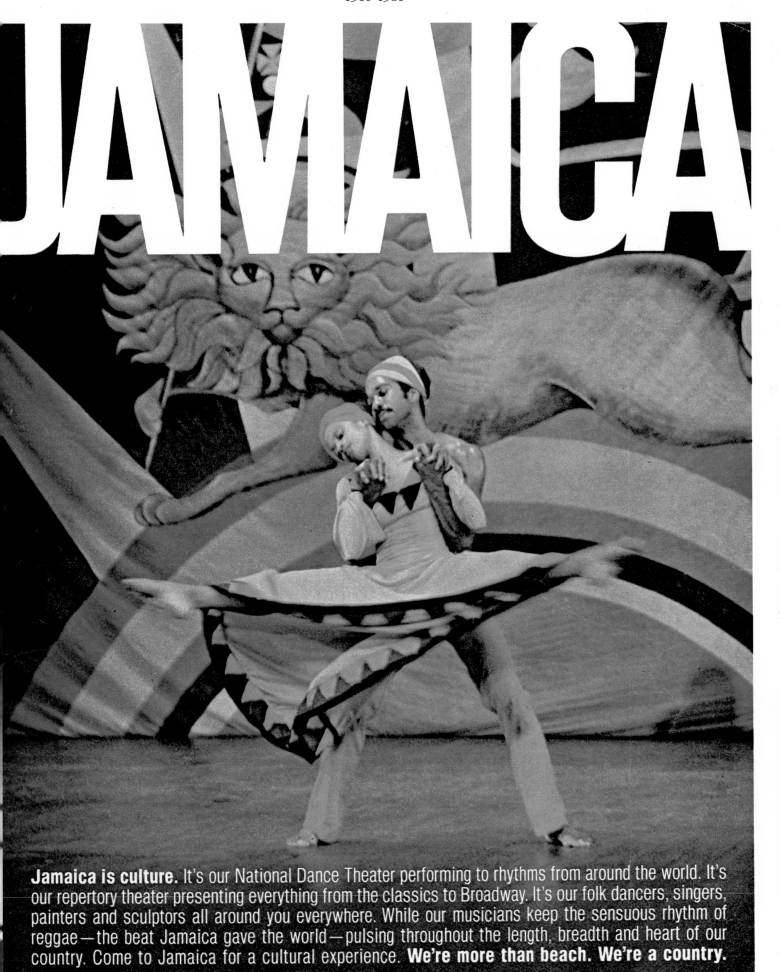

JAMAICA

Jamaica is culture. It's our National Dance Theater performing to rhythms from around the world. It's our repertory theater presenting everything from the classics to Broadway. It's our folk dancers, singers, painters and sculptors all around you everywhere. While our musicians keep the sensuous rhythm of reggae—the beat Jamaica gave the world—pulsing throughout the length, breadth and heart of our country. Come to Jamaica for a cultural experience. **We're more than beach. We're a country.**

©JAMAICA TOURIST BOARD 1979

Jamaica. Ad. Robert Freson. 1980. Jamaica Tourist Board

Live in peace with your pipe.
Benson & Hedges Mellow Virginia.

Benson & Hedges Mellow Virginia. Ad. 1973.
Benson and Hedges Ltd

Bisquit Cognac. Ad. John Jensen. 1979. J. R. Parkington Ltd

John Wanamaker, department store. Ad.
John and Linda Gist. 1976. John Wanamaker

Time magazine. Cover. Edward Sorel. 1980. © Time Inc

Wideband, gold coin jewelry. Ad. Cosimo. 1979.
Wideband Corporation

NAPIER
IS
SAUCIER.
Clip or pierced earrings, $11.00, and $12.00.

Napier jewelry. Ad. William Helburn. © 1979.
The Napier Co

Johnnie Walker Red. Ad. John Rettallack.
1977. Somerset Importers, Ltd

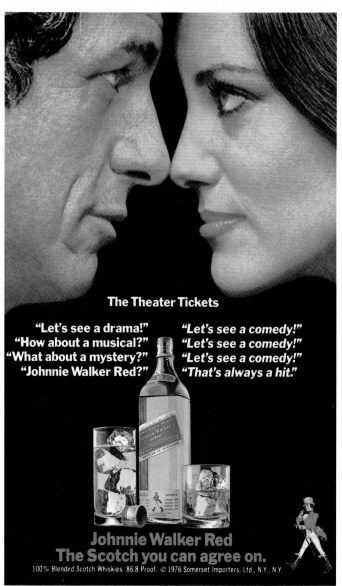

Bracelets, ring and earrings from the **Christian Dior** Jewelry Collection by **Grossé**.
About $50. At Bonwit Teller, Saks, I. Magnin, and other fine stores.

CHRIS VON WANGENHEIM

Fetching is Your Dior.

Christian Dior, jewelry by Grossé. Ad. Chris Von Wangenheim. 1976. Christian Dior, New York

Only those who dare... truly live

For the name of the authorized Ferrari dealer nearest you, call these numbers toll-free: (800)447-4700 or, in Illinois, (800)322-4400.

Ferrari

Only those who dare . . . truly live. Ad. Bob Bender. 1980. Ferrari

White Horse whiskey: 'Scotch and American'. Ad (detail). Nick Hazzard. 1978. White Horse Distillers Ltd

'Powerhouse', recording by American Tears. Album cover (detail). Robert Giusti. 1978. CBS Inc

LEFT:
Sony Records. Calendar design (detail). John O'Leary. 1975.
Sony Corp of America

OPPOSITE:
Smirnoff Vodka. Ad. Tony Whetton/Brian Duffy. 1974.
International Distillers & Vintners Ltd

"Well, they said anything could happen."

Remember, whatever happens don't overdo it.

"UN BAR AUX FOLIES-BERGERES" BY STEVE CAMPBELL FROM MANET.

Ogilvy&Mather

Campari. Reflection on art.

Campari aperitif. Ad. Steve Campbell. 1980. Austin, Nichols & Co., Inc

ACKNOWLEDGMENTS

The author wishes to express his sincere thanks to the companies, artists, and photographers whose names appear under the illustrations in this book, as well as to the advertising agencies, listed below, who throughout the years have also been extremely generous in submitting material for editorial use in Studio Books—particularly in the annual, *Modern Publicity* (for which the author was American editor while Director of Studio Books at The Viking Press). Special thanks are also due to David Herbert, John Smith, Felix Gluck, and to Studio-Vista for making their libraries and files available, also to the History of Advertising Trust, The Victoria & Albert Museum, The Royal Society of Arts, The London Museum, The British Transport Museum, The National Motor Museum, The Bodleian Library, and The Imperial War Museum; to Le Musée des Arts Decoratifs, Musée Grévin, and The Paris Opera Library; to The Metropolitan Museum of Art, The Museum of Modern Art, The New-York Historical Society, The New York Public Library, The American Federation of Art, The Library of Congress, The Institute of Outdoor Advertising, The Art Directors Club of New York, The Lincoln Center for the Performing Arts, The Phillips Gallery, and The Coffee House Club.

For their helpful suggestions and contacts he is also grateful to the stylist, Yvonne McHarg, to Terence Brown of The Society of Illustrators, and to Mrs. Joseph Binder; to Cary Boyd and Sandra A. Sutliff of Doyle Dane Bernbach, and, most particularly, to Meredith A. Young of Compton Advertising, who put in many hours of valuable research on behalf of this book.

Very special thanks are also due to the legendary Charles Pick of William Heinemann Ltd, whose idea this book was in the first place, and to Nigel Hollis and Brenda Rouse, also of Heinemann; to Mary Velthoven, his deeply respected editor at Viking Penguin, and Shirley Brownrigg, the copy editor only the luckiest of authors will find, to Carol Sue Leslie and to Barbara Burn who as editor of Studio Books in New York has carried on the tradition started in London in 1893 by Charles Holme, from whose original collection many of the illustrations in this book have been taken. He is also deeply indebted to Christopher Holme for the design of the book, and to Gloria MacDonald, Frank Grant, Frederic Bradlee, Harry and Claudia Lennon, Dorry Richardson, and Anne Dumas for their invaluable assistance and encouragement.

ADVERTISING AGENCIES

Abbott Kimball; Advertising and Publicity; Aitken-Kynett Company; Carl Ally; Altman, Stoller & Chalk; Altman, Stoller, Weiss Advertising; R. Anderson Advertising; Anderson & Cairns; N. W. Ayer; L. Banks; Batten, Barton, Durstine & Osborne; Bartable Advertising and Marketing; Batsford, Constantine & Gardner; The Baynard Press; John Belknap; S. H. Benson; Benton & Bowles; R. H. E. W. Bernard; The Biow Company; The Blaine-Thompson Co.; The Blackman Co; Bozell & Jacobs; T. B. Browne; Brownstone Associates; Leo Burnett & Company; Calkins & Holden; Campbell-Ewald; Carlton Advertising; A. A. Casmir; C. R. Casson; Cecil & Presbrey; Central Advertising Service; Chermayeff & Geismar Associates; City & General; Clifford Bloxham & Partners; Clowes Advertising; Cluett, Peabody; Collett, Dickenson & Pearce & Partners; Colman, Prentis & Varley; Compton Advertising; Cornell, May & Stevenson; W. S. Crawford; Geo. Cuming; Cunningham & Walsh; Dancer Fitzgerald Sample; Daniel & Charles Associates; D'Arcy Advertising; DeGarmo, McCaffery; Paul E. Derrick; Dixon's West End; Dodge-Delano; Doherty, Clifford, Steers & Shenfield; Donahue & Associates; Dorland Advertising; Doyle Dane & Bernbach; Roy S. Durstine; W. H. Emmett; John Engred; Erwin-Wasey; William Esty Company; Everetts Advertising; Federal Advertising; J. R. Flanagan Advertising; Fletchard Richard; Foote, Cone & Belding; Hank Forssberg; Clinton E. Frank; Freeman, Matthews & Milne; French, Guillenden, Osborn; Fuller, Smith & Ross; Gardner, Sullivan, Stouffer; S. T. Garland Advertising Service; Gibbons-O'Neill; Gilbert Advertising; Gore, Smith & Greenland; Grant Advertising; Greenly's; Grey Advertising; Group One Creative Graphics; Lawrence C. Gumbinner Advertising; Gumbinner-North Co; John Haddon; The Heritage-Peters Advertising; Hicks & Greist; Charles F. Higham; Charles W. Hobson; The Laurance Holman Advertising Service; Haward E. Edrick Advertising; Hudson & Morrison; Interlink Advertising; Intermarco-Farner Advertising; Jacobson Advertising; Kenyon & Eckhardt; The Kleppner Co; Kudner Agency; Kudner-Compton; C. J. La Roche Co; Lennen & Mitchell; Lennen, Newell & Wolsey; Lloyd Chester & Dillingham; London Press Exchange; Lord, Geller, Frederico, Einstein; Lord & Thomas; Lyman Simpson; C. J. Lytle & Royds; McCann-Erickson; MacManus, John & Adams; David Malked; Marketing Directions; The Marschalk Company; Clifford Martin; Mather & Crowther; J. M. Mathes; Maxon; H. K. McCann; Robert Miles Runyon Associates; Morton Freund Advertising; Muller, Blatchley & Co; Nadler & Larimer; Nash & Alexander; Needham, Harper & Steers; Needham, Louis & Brorby; Newell-Emmett; Norman, Craig & Kummel; Norton Simon; Cecil D. Notley Advertising; Ogilvy, Benson & Mather; O'Grady, Anderson & Gray; Robert W. Orr & Associates; The Osborne-Peacock Co; Osborne, Royds & Co; A. J. Owen; Paris & Peart; Jerome Parker Agency; Pedlar & Ryan; Alfred Pemberton; F. C. Pritchard Wood & Partners; Push Pin Studios; Reach, McClinton & Co; Regent Advertising Service; Peter Rogers, Associates; Rosebud Studio; Ross Roy-Fogarty; Rowlinson-Broughton; G. S. Royds; Rumble Crowther & Nicholas; Runyan & Associates; Saward Baker Co; Charles Schlaifer & Co; Service Advertising Co; Douglas Sisnon Agency; Smees; Smith-Greenland; Franklin Spier; Leonard Stein; Stephens Advertising & A. Pemberton; Sterling Advertising; Stewart Alexander Advertising; G. Street & Co; Stuart Advertising; John Tait & Partners; Tatham-Laird & Kudner; J. Walter Thompson Co; A. Tolmer; C. Vernon & Sons; Vernon Stratton; Vickers & Benson; Warwick & Legler; Wasey-Campbell-Ewald; Weber, Geiger & Kalat; William H. Weintraub Company; Wells, Rich, Greene; Martin Williams Advertising; Wills; Fred Wittner Advertising; The Winter, Thomas Co; Wunderman, Ricotta & Kline; Young & Rubicam.

In addition, thanks are due to Thomas Barker & Sons, and R. P. Gossop.

INDEX
to the illustrations

Illustration by Edward Bawden
for Shell-Mex. 1936